Better Golf in Six Swings

Better Golf in Six Swings

by Dick Aultman

A GOLF DIGEST BOOK

Published by Golf Digest/Tennis, Inc.,
A New York Times Company,
495 Westport Avenue,
P.O. Box 5350,
Norwalk, Connecticut 06856

Trade book distribution by
Simon and Schuster
A Division of Gulf + Western Industries, Inc.
New York, New York 10020

First Printing
ISBN: 0-914178-51-2
Library of Congress: 82-80147
Manufactured in the
United States of America

Cover and book design by Dorothy Geiser.
Printing and binding by R.R. Donnelley & Sons.

Contents

SHORT GAME SHORTCUTS

Dick Aultman

Instinctive break-throughs

The title of this book implies gimmickry, "Band-Aid" cures that seldom last beyond the front nine. "Anything to sell copies," you well might say, especially if you've struggled for years to cure your slice or build a useful swing that works repeatedly.

True, no one has ever excelled at golf without spending thousands of hours striking balls and stroking putts. Jack Grout, the man who has taught Jack Nicklaus since he started his amazing career at age 10, estimates it takes *at least* five years of all but daily dedication to become a quality player. He may be right.

On the other hand, I firmly believe that it is possible to create a *breakthrough* in one's golfing development in just a few swings of the club. I've seen it happen countless times.

The player whose drives usually curve weakly from left to right suddenly bores them straight down the fairway or draws them slightly from right to center.

The player who has always muscled the ball to little avail, with knuckles white and veins popping from his forearms, stares in wonder after striking his career tee shot with what felt to be an effortless swing.

The pupil who has too often skulled his wedge shots low and hot across the green suddenly discovers that they actually fly high and settle softly when, of all things, he tries to make them fly *lower*.

Often these are not breakthroughs. They are fluke occurrences, a rare combination of "wrongs" that happen to produce an immaculate "right"—once. They may not reoccur in similar combination before the next sighting of Halley's Comet.

A true and lasting breakthrough occurs when:

1. The golfer can feel what he did to create the successful shot.

2. He has a way to recapture that feeling in the future.

Each chapter in this book is designed to create

certain feelings within you, to either cure a specific problem you may have with your shots or to generally upgrade your shotmaking skills.

Moreover, you will be given a way to discover these feelings quickly—hence the book's title—and *instinctively*, through doing what comes naturally.

So often in golf our instincts create problems. When the ball sits on the ground, for instance, they tell us to help it up. So we top it on the upswing and it dribbles along the ground. This result strengthens the urge to help it up, which leads to further topping.

When we see our shots slicing to the right, we instinctively swing more to the left, which leads to more slicing and other problems as well.

When we want to drive the ball far, we instinctively hold on tighter and swing harder and faster. Wrong again.

The standard approach for correcting bad shots is to attempt some changes in our preswing and inswing techniques. These changes are usually designed, in effect, to overcome the instincts that have led us astray. Often, however, the suggested corrections are so numerous, or so complex, or so anti-instinctive that our minds and bodies cannot accept them at all, or only over a period of months or years.

The approach in this book will be to cultivate and direct your instincts, rather than sublimate them.

But we will cultivate those instincts to make them productive for golf.

I will do this by asking you to put yourself into unusual shotmaking situations or to perform some other unusual feat. The situation or the feat will, in itself, force you to react in certain ways. Your reactions will be instinctive, but probably correct.

You will be asked to sense what you feel as you perform successfully in these situations, so that you can repeat the feel—and the success—on normal golf shots.

If you should happen to lose the feeling that created success, you'll be able to recapture it at any time by merely re-creating the unusual situation that caused you to experience it in the first place.

I should point out that there is good news and bad news about trying to improve your game this way. The good news first:

1. It saves time. You strike better shots sooner because you bypass many conscious changes that would take time to perfect. (Actually, you will make many changes as you react to the situations I'll put you in, but you will make them without trying. Often you will not realize you've made them.)

2. It reduces conscious effort and lets you perform naturally. We have a tremendous amount of natural ability within us. However, too much mental direction—too much trying—disallows our using it. For

instance, you may have surprised yourself on numerous occasions when you casually, without thinking, backhanded a meaningless putt directly into the hole—a putt that you know you might well have missed if you'd really been trying to sink it.

3. It is an approach that works on the course, not just on the practice tee. Golfers play their best when they play by feel, when they somehow sense beforehand how their swing should feel to create the shot they want to make. Too much trying creates mental and physical tensions that stifle our ability to sense how our swing should feel and to swing accordingly.

Now, the bad news:

1. This approach requires that you select and apply yourself to only those situations that fit your particular needs. Many chapters in this book will not apply to you. For instance, if your problem is hooking the ball to the left with a closed clubface, you would merely compound that problem by pursuing my anti-slice suggestions, designed to correct for an open clubface.

To avoid this happening, I will clarify what the instruction is meant to correct or improve generally. Often I will describe the typical bad shots of a player who needs the particular type of help being covered therein. It will be up to you to decide if that shot pattern does or does not apply to you. If not, do not try to apply the advice, though you may wish to read the chapter for pleasure and enlightenment.

2. It is important that the adjustments in your technique that result from your performing in the unusual situation be fundamentally correct. We don't want to create mere compensations, more wrongs to offset other wrongs.

To avoid this happening, I have done two things. First, I've limited the scope of the instruction to only those areas where your instinctive reactions are likely to be fundamentally correct. Second, I have included some instructional guidance, some things to do to help you feel what you should feel. The things I suggest, however, will be few in number and easy to do. We will avoid mental and physical paralysis at all cost.

Apart from trying to help you play better golf sooner, and thus enjoy this wonderful game more, I have a second purpose in writing this book. It is to introduce you to many of the excellent instructors I have observed, taught with and written books for.

I think you will enjoy reading about these men and the fascinating, innovative means they have used to help golfers like yourself play better.

Indeed, a vast portion of the instruction herein stems directly or indirectly from my association with these teachers, and their unfailing willingness to share their knowledge and experience with me.

Finally, I would also like to thank my friends at

Golf Digest magazine for letting me teach in their instruction school program since 1971, an experience that has taken me to some of the country's finest golf resorts, exposed me to some of its finest teachers and brought me into contact, both on and off the course, with thousands of its most interested and interesting golfers.

—Dick Aultman
Weston, Connecticut
June 1982

Full-Swing Shortcuts

Bob Toski

1

If your gorilla swing takes you
into the jungle. . . .

Lob some pennies to lighten your touch

If an opinion poll were taken to determine America's best-known teacher of golf, Bob Toski would dominate the balloting as surely as he dominates any lesson tee on which he works.

Sam Snead calls him "Mouse" because of his smallish size—5'-7", 127 pounds. But during a lesson Bob will roar like a lion, purr like a kitten or push and shove like an elephant, depending on what it takes to put the pupil's mind and body into the proper frame for shooting lower scores.

During one particular lesson at Palmetto Dunes on

Hilton Head Island, S.C., the pupil's swing affliction was a particularly tight right arm. To relax the arm, Toski first tried grazing it lightly with his fingertips.

"Feel that?" he asked.

"Yes," the pupil replied. But then he continued to swing with the arm all but rigid.

So Bob next leaned over and gently kissed his right arm.

"Feel that?"

Again the pupil replied affirmatively, but still the offending arm failed to fold during his backswing.

Finally, Toski took the arm in his hands, brought it to his mouth, and clamped down with his teeth.

"Feel THAT?" Toski asked as the pupil yelped in pain.

Bob did make his point. The pupil did discover some right-arm sensitivity. And following the lesson he proudly displayed his badge of courage, the imprint of Toski's teeth in the meaty part of his forearm.

No two Toski lessons are the same. He tailors each session to meet the individual's own unique psychological and physical strengths and weaknesses. Over the years, however, two distinct convictions have evolved from his efforts to help golfers improve.

The first is that, ideally, golf should be learned from the green outward. Build your technique, and your confidence, on a foundation of holing short putts. Then move on, gradually, to longer swings with longer clubs.

Toski's second teaching theme is that most bad shots stem in large part from overcontrolling the club with the hands—flipping it, twisting it, grabbing it, shoving it. All tend to misalign and/or misdirect the clubhead.

And each form of overcontrol requires some degree of unwarranted grip pressure. The hold on the club is either too tight just prior to swinging, or there's an in-swing spasm thereafter.

A light grip from start to finish lets the arms swing freely and rhythmically. It is by far the better tactic for creating both clubhead speed and solid contact.

For most players, however, it is highly unnatural to hold the club lightly. All past experience with creating powerful blows seems to dictate a tight grip from the start or a switch from light to tight somewhere along the way.

Retaining a light grip all the way through impact, especially with the distance clubs, requires sublimating the fear that the club will surely escape from the hands and go twirling down the fairway. It demands a monumental degree of trust, like hiring a John Dillinger to guard your bank.

Few are immune to the tendency to overcontrol the club. More than once Toski has told a surgeon-pupil that, "if you handle the scalpel like you hold

21

that club, I think I'd look for a second opinion."

Thus it is that Bob prefers the putting green as the starting place for building de-control. There, even the gorilla golfer can abide a constantly light grip, because he senses that *exact* distance, not *maximum* distance, is the goal.

There he can learn to identify what a light grip feels like and begin to appreciate its benefits. He not only starts sinking more putts, but he also begins to sense that if light gripping leads to solid contact on the green, it just might improve his impact on full shots as well.

A quick and simple way to discover how a constantly light grip should feel is to lob coins underhanded into a wastebasket or box that you have set on a carpet in your home.

You will find that this is difficult to do well, consistently, if you hold the coin tightly in your fingers, or if you flip your wrist instead of swing your arm.

The better way is to lay the coin atop your forefinger and middle finger, near the tips (see illustration). Then merely swing your arm back and forward toward the target. Let the coin simply float off your fingers.

Try to sense that your arm is relaxed throughout the motion it makes. Swing it smoothly, rhythmically without hurry.

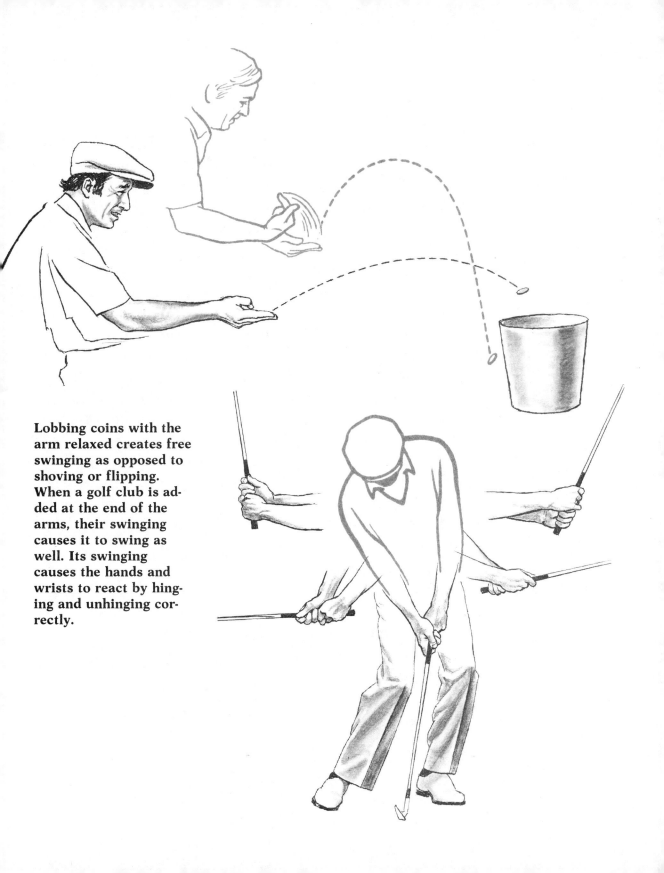

Lobbing coins with the arm relaxed creates free swinging as opposed to shoving or flipping. When a golf club is added at the end of the arms, their swinging causes it to swing as well. Its swinging causes the hands and wrists to react by hinging and unhinging correctly.

After just a few tries, you should also sense that the distance the coin flies depends solely on the distance that the arm swings, with no influence whatsoever from the wrist or finger joints.

The final step is to actually putt some balls across the carpet or a putting green. Start with short putts. Don't worry if they miss your target. Your only goal is to recapture the feeling of relaxed lightness in your right hand and arm, throughout each swing, that you sensed when lobbing the coins.

When you succeed, the contact should feel solid. The ball should feel light as it comes off the putter-face.

Once the contact becomes solid consistently, as it should after just a few tries, gradually move farther from the target with the putter and, eventually, into chipping, then pitching and, finally, full swings.

Do not try to increase your grip pressure, however. Try to hold the club lightly throughout each swing. To make the ball fly a greater distance, merely lengthen the distance that your arms swing back and forward.

As your swings lengthen, the weight of the moving club will cause your wrists to hinge and unhinge. This is normal and desirable for creating both club-head speed and solid contact.

However, hinging and unhinging should happen naturally as a *reaction* to the swing. It will if you

24

continue to hold the club lightly. The only way to inhibit wrist action, or to make it take place at the wrong time, is to tighten your grip before or during your swing.

Unfortunately, because such tightening is so instinctive, it is bound to reoccur. When it does, before your next shot, merely swing your right arm back and forth at your side. Simulate the motion you made, and the feeling you had, when lobbing the pennies.

Jack Grout

2

If you enjoy long courses, but wish the fairways were twice as wide . . .

Quiet your hands with a 3-finger grip

Jack Grout is a kindly, soft-spoken gentle man who much prefers sinking his teeth into fresh clams rather than pupils' forearms.

He was head professional at Scioto Country Club, Columbus, Ohio, in 1950 when a new member named Charlie Nicklaus asked if he'd mind letting his son, Jackie, enroll in the junior classes that Grout was conducting.

"He's only 10," Mr. Nicklaus told Grout, "but he likes sports and seems to have some athletic ability."

Thus began a teacher-pupil relationship, and a warm friendship, that remains intact 30 years later.

In 1974 Nicklaus would write a foreword to Grout's instruction book, *Let Me Teach You Golf As I Taught Jack Nicklaus:*

"I can assure you," Nicklaus said, "that the simplicity of Jack Grout's approach is *the* major reason why I've managed to play as well as I have over the years. Along with my parents and my wife, he has been the biggest and surely the best influence in my life."

Evidence of Grout's simplistic approach came through many times during the course of my helping him write his book. One sunny February morning we were driving up from Miami to North Palm Beach where he was to spend the afternoon coaching Nicklaus, checking out his entire game for the upcoming spring competitions. The particular topic that Grout was discussing as he drove the car was the role of the hands in the golf swing.

"The hands are a necessary evil in golf," he said into my tape recorder. "You need them to hold onto the club, but beyond that they usually do more harm than good. The best thing you can do with them is nothing. Just hold on lightly and let them react to the movement of the club."

Some time later while reflecting on Grout's succinct appraisal, I recalled an earlier observation made by another Ohio-based professional, Jim Flick. During the course of selecting photographs for his book, *Square-to-Square Golf in Pictures,* Jim and I were looking over a sequence of photos showing Nicklaus swinging a driver. Flick, whose interest in the golf swing borders on obsession, all but leaped from his chair.

"See that," he exclaimed. "His fingers are off the club."

Indeed, in the particular photo that showed Nicklaus at impact, swinging his longest club in the neighborhood of 120 miles per hour, his right thumb and forefinger were actually apart from the club-shaft. The student, Nicklaus, was doing with his hands what his teacher, Grout, had advocated from the start—nothing.

As mentioned in the preceding chapter, submitting the hands to a passive role requires extreme trust. Nicklaus himself has written that "keeping those limelight-hoggers backstage . . . was the hardest thing of all for me to learn."

One quick and simple way to discover if your hands are overcontrolling your swing is to simply apply, throughout your swing, what the Nicklaus photo showed him doing at impact.

Take your favorite club within the 5-iron to 7-iron range and place the ball on a low tee. Grip the club and address the ball as you normally do. Then, just prior to swinging, spread your right thumb and forefinger apart so that neither touches the club, but not so wide that you feel tension in your forearm. In fact, your right arm, especially, should always feels soft as you prepare to swing.

Maintain this grip throughout your swing.

Your initial sensation might be that you are swinging with insufficient control over the club. Fine. The purpose of the drill is, in fact, to tone down the hands' control and to thus allow the club to swing freely, as the manufacturer built it to do.

If the seeming loss of control makes you hesitant to swing as aggressively as you normally might, so much the better. For most golfers, a bit less physical effort improves the quality of the contact and thus makes shots go farther.

If this grip improves your shots, continue applying it on alternate swings during your practice sessions until you can consistently retain a light grip throughout your entire swing when you hold the club in your normal fashion. Feel free to apply this training grip, as needed, during actual play as well.

This training grip is for golfers who frequently misconnect with the ball because their hands overcontrol the club. If its application does not improve your shots within a short period of practice, chances are good that too much hand action is not your particular problem.

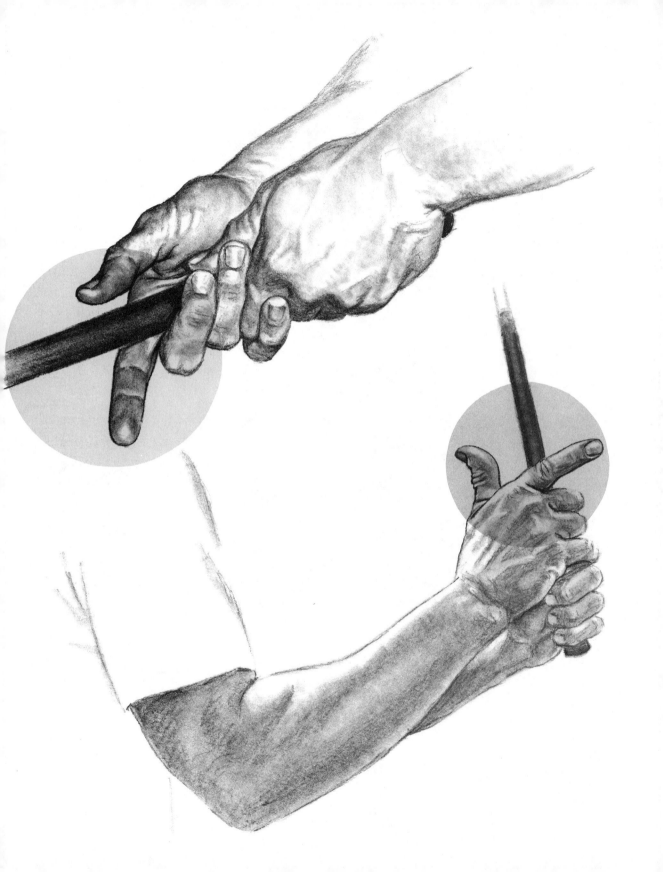

John Jacobs

If your ball tends to curve too
far to the right, it may be too far
to the left at address . . .

Play ball to the right to curve it left

It is early morning on the driving range at an exclusive golf resort. There is a nip in the air, but sunlight sparkles off the moist grass, foretelling a warm day ahead.

The teeing area is wide, lush and newly-mowed, as yet unblemished by divot marks. Across this emerald expanse, piles of shiny white balls form glistening pyramids at carefully spaced intervals.

They await the students, some 40 men and women who are now seated on a group of chairs facing down the range. These are avid golfers of widely varying abilities. They have come from all over the world to learn to play the game correctly, once and for all, hang the expense. For the next five days they will be taught by John Jacobs, premier British instructor, and his staff.

Jacobs is a tall, slightly stooped Yorkshireman with thick wavy hair and a deep professorial voice. A winner among losers on the 1955 British Ryder Cup team, he has since become the best-known golf instructor in the United Kingdom and Europe, with growing influence in the United States as well.

This influence is reflected by American teachers' increasing emphasis on what have become known as "impact factors," or ball-flight "laws" or "influences." Simply stated, John's message over the years has been that improved ball-striking requires improving what the club is doing when it meets the ball. Its path of movement in relation to the target line; its face alignment in relation to its path; its angle of approach—downward, upward or level—and its speed all determine the ball's flight pattern.

That flight pattern tells you if you've succeeded or failed, of course. But more importantly, it can tell you why. It reveals which impact factor(s) need some attention.

"The ball is your best teacher," Jacobs has said many times. "It never lies."

When it comes to relating shot patterns to impact factors, and impact factors to human causes, Jacobs is a supreme diagnostician. His opening clinic at a golf school clearly demonstrates this fact.

Jacobs first asks for a volunteer student to be taught in front of the group, someone he has never seen swing a club.

Most of the students shrink down into their windbreakers, fearful of such exposure, but a few do raise their hands. The man chosen finds his driver and steps forward.

Jacobs watches as the pupil tees a ball. Then John walks forward to the front of the tee and off to one side. He faces down the range, away from the student.

He will teach the player without watching him swing.

The first shot dribbles along the ground, a bit off to the left. The next flies low to the left and then curves weakly back to the center of the range. The third try also bends from left to right.

Jacobs has seen enough. Still without looking back at the pupil, he asks one of his assistants to alter the player's ball positioning, to adjust his shoulder alignment and to give his grip a "tweek" to the right.

From these new positions the pupil tries again. This time the ball flies straight down the center of the range. It rolls well beyond the earlier attempts.

"Well done," John exclaims. "Now let's try one more."

Before the next shot, Jacobs asks his assistant to see that the student accentuates slightly the various pre-swing adjustments just prescribed.

This time the ball starts out a bit to the right and then draws back to center, rolling still farther down the range.

The pupil is astonished, and delighted. In just five swings, on a cool morning with no warmup shots, he's just learned to curve the ball from right to left for, as he later admits, the first time in his golfing career.

And from a teacher who never watched him swing.

I have watched Jacobs perform this demonstration many times, occasionally serving as his assistant. The pupils' problems vary from clinic to clinic, as do his corrective measures. Not once did I see him fail to improve a student's shots in just a few tries.

The demonstration captures the group's attention, of course. Its main purpose, however, is to show the class members that they, too, can benefit through a better understanding of how various types of ball flight can reveal just which impact factors need improvement.

The problem that Jacobs corrected in this particular instance is extremely common. More golfers than not do, in fact, find their long shots starting out to

36

the left and then curving weakly to the right. This happens because the club is *moving* toward the left of target when it strikes the ball, but it is *facing* to the right of that path.

If this is your shotmaking tendency, you might benefit from making the same preswing adjustments that John actually prescribed for this particular student. They were:

1. Play the ball farther back to the right in your stance, several inches in fact. It will seem that the ball is considerably closer to your right foot than your left.

2. Align your shoulders well to the right. You will feel that you have partially turned your back to the target prior to swinging, and that you will surely start the ball off to the right.

3. Grip the club with your hands turned slightly more to the right, a bit clockwise from your norm.

Having made these three adjustments, it should be easier for you to visualize the imaginary path shown in the illustration on the following pages. This path bisects the ball from "4 o'clock" to "10 o'clock."

One of your goals should be to swing the club into the ball along this path, which is admittedly toward right of target.

Your other goal should be to turn the club to the left, counterclockwise, throughout your downswing so that it faces to the left of its path of movement at

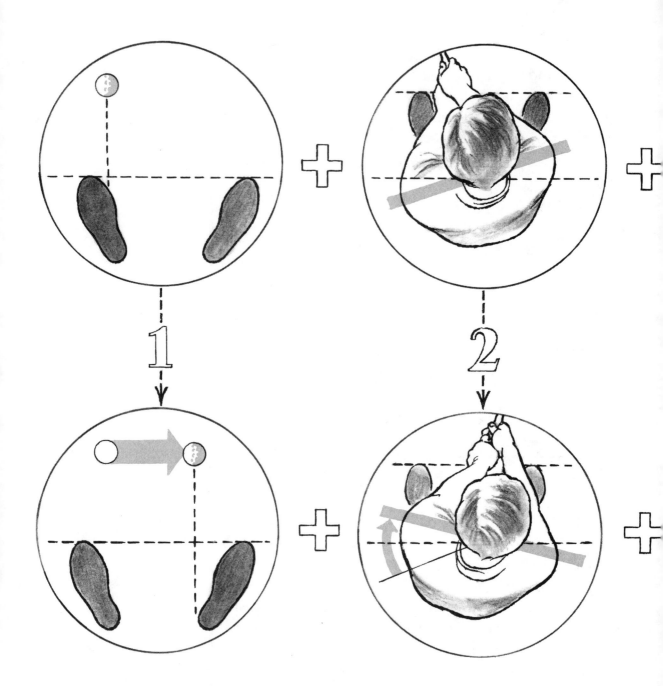

Anti-slice adjustments are shown in the bottom row of illustrations, in contrast to the slice-creating positions shown atop. Pre-swing corrections include (1) ball positioned farther back to the right, (2) shoulders aligned somewhat to the right and (3) hands turned to the right (clockwise). These adjustments are meant to create an in-to-out clubhead path with the club facing a bit to the left of that path during impact.

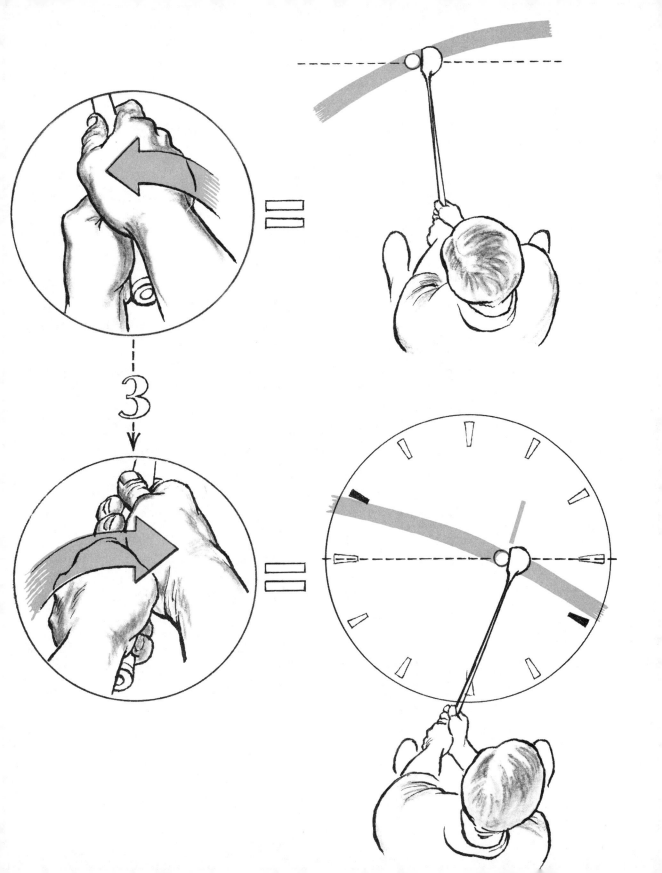

3

impact. You should do this turning with your arms and hands, not with your shoulders.

When you accomplish these goals, the ball will start out to the right—that being the club's path—and then curve to the left—that being where the club is facing.

Since you will probably be without face-to-face supervision, I suggest that initially you play these shots with a 5-iron or 6-iron and with the ball setting on a low tee. These shorter clubs are easier to turn to the left during the downswing by using the arms and hands rather than the shoulders.

Also, you may find that it is easier to so turn the club if you start with your feet and hips also aligned to the right.

Yes, these preswing adjustments are, in fact, over-corrections. They will probably seem more extreme than they really are, however, if you have been playing the ball too far forward to the left and thus been forced to turn your shoulders and hands too far to the left in order to set the clubhead behind it.

But these extreme positions are temporary, designed merely to make you feel a different clubhead path and a freer turning of the club to the left during your downswing. Once your shots do begin to curve abruptly from right to left, it will be time to gradually retrace your steps back to a more orthodox ball position, shoulder alignment and grip.

Old habits die hard, however, so always be alert

40

against regressing back to your former positions. The warning signs will be long shots that bend from left to right and, perhaps, full wedge and 9-iron shots that start left and continue left without curving to the right.

Finally, I should stress that these are all anti-slice adjustments, designed to eliminate impact that finds the club moving left of target and facing right of that path. If your long shots already curve from right to left, or from center to left, these changes would merely aggravate that leftward curve.

41

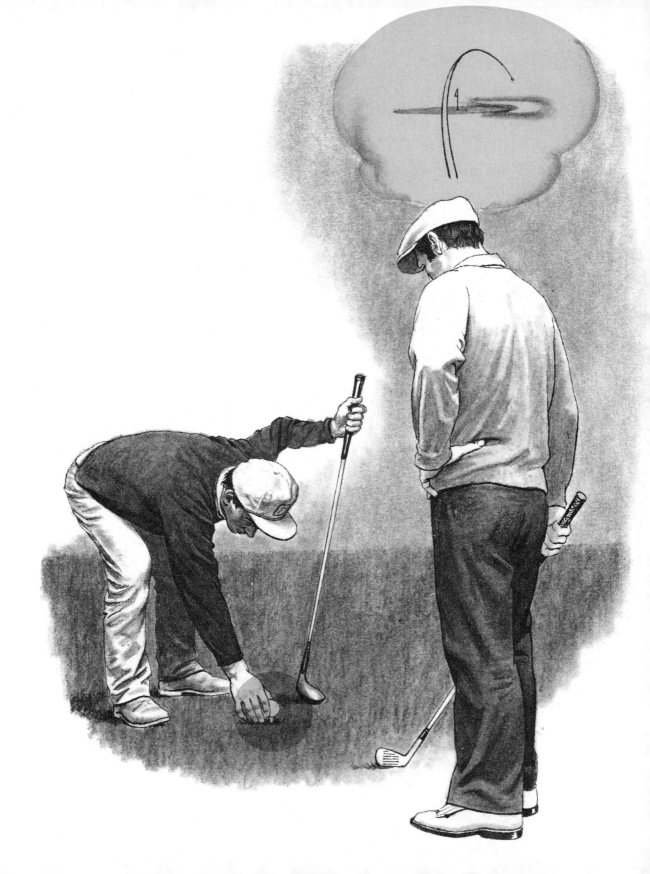

If you now tee the ball too high
or too low, the peg you are
using may be merely a crutch . . .

Tee higher or lower to improve your path

Most teachers tee the ball or move it onto a preferred lie for the pupil. Some, however, like to let the student perform this act, at least early in the lesson. They know that the height that the golfer prefers to tee the ball can reveal a great deal about his or her swing tendencies.

A given player will habitually tee the ball more or less the same height every time, unless he's an expert planning to play a certain type of tee shot or a beginner who has not yet developed a pattern.

And the teeing height that the player prefers will

depend largely on the type of contact he tends to make on his *bad* shots. He will instinctively tee the ball to a height that best allows him to make fairly decent contact despite the flaws in his technique. He will use the height of the tee as a crutch to minimize disaster.

For instance, it is common for golfers to tee the ball low if they tend to chop downward, with the clubhead moving into the striking area on an extremely steep angle of approach. Their instincts tell them that they might chop under a high-teed ball and pop it up. Teeing it low all but precludes this happening.

Unfortunately, using this crutch tends to prolong and strengthen the chopping tendency. When the ball is teed low, the golfer dare not swing the clubhead into it on a level or slightly upward angle of approach, even though this is preferable on tee shots with the woods. With the ball teed low, a level or upward approach risks catching turf behind the ball and/or striking only its upper portion.

Conversely, teeing the ball fairly high is favored among players who do tend to sweep it away with a level or upward-moving clubhead. This approach is ideal for driving the ball long distances, because the force of the blow is applied forward instead of downward. Since most touring professionals do swing slightly upward to the ball on their drives, they do, in fact, tend to tee the ball high.

Among less-skilled amateurs, however, teeing the ball high often indicates that a problem will arise when they must play shots from the fairway without the benefit of the peg. They lack the pros' ability to adjust and strike with a somewhat descending blow when the ball is on the grass. Instead they create the same level or upward approach as befits them on the tee. Unless the ball sets up high on the fairway grass, they will tend to scrape turf behind it, or to catch it thin or top it. These players thrive on "winter rules," which allows nudging or placing the ball onto a nearby tuft of grass.

For these players, using the crutch of teeing the ball high merely prolongs and strengthens the swing problems that put them at a loss when they must play from a normal or tight lie in the fairway or the rough.

The main point to be made here is that many golfers can improve through practice with the ball setting at a height that, initially, is not to their liking. By taking away the crutch that helps them get away with making inferior swings, they can force themselves to make better swings and better shots.

This improvement happens more or less instinctively, without conscious effort to change some aspect of their technique. The mind and body sense what must be done to accommodate the new, albeit forced, situation. They react accordingly, and correctly.

Specifically, if you tend to undercut and pop up your drives, practice with the ball teed high. Try to sweep the ball away without dislodging the peg. Sense how your swing feels when you succeed, especially the path on which the club is moving.

This practice is also excellent for players who frequently pull-slice long shots from left to right and pull their approach shots to the left with the shorter irons.

If you now tee the ball quite high, you might benefit from practicing 4-wood or 5-wood shots with the ball setting down in the grass or resting on bare

Golfers who swing steeply downward to the ball on drives generally tee it unusually low (left-hand illustrations) to avoid undercutting it. They also tend to swing on a too-upright plane that can lead to pull-slicing shots from left to right. Teeing higher forces them to create a flatter, more sweeping approach to avoid undercutting. Added distance should result.

Those who tee the ball high may do so to avoid catching turf behind it or topping it on the upswing. These tendencies result from their swing path being from too far inside the target line. This path can also lead to hooking. Teeing the ball lower, or practicing from bare ground with a 4-wood or 5-wood, will help improve their swing path and angle of approach. They will begin to improve their contact, not only on drives but also on shots from grass.

 LOW

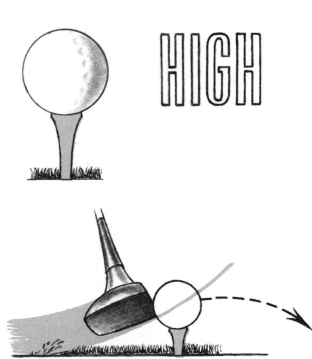 HIGH

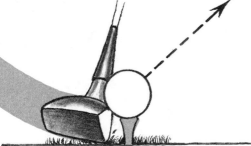

If you do this. . .

If you do this. . .

. . .and this. . .

. . .and this. . .

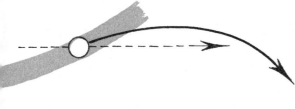

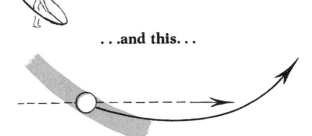

. . .tee the
   ball higher

. . .tee the
   ball lower.

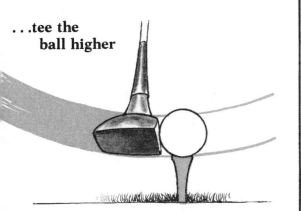

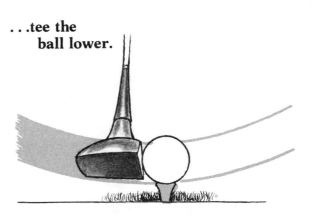

ground. This would certainly be helpful if your shot-making pattern includes pushing the ball to the right on a straight line, hooking from right to left and/or failing to achieve normal height with the driver.

In fact, if this happens to be your pattern, it is quite probable that you've already stowed your driver in some dark closet, to do penance for producing all those nosediving, wormburning shots that so often darted into trouble on the left.

For you, especially, practicing off bare ground with your 4-wood or 5-wood might produce some ugly shots at first. With time and patience, however, this regimen might well lead to your actually bringing the naughty No. 1 wood back to life, as well as to better contact on your iron shots.

In the meantime, I suggest you also resist the temptation to play winter rules.

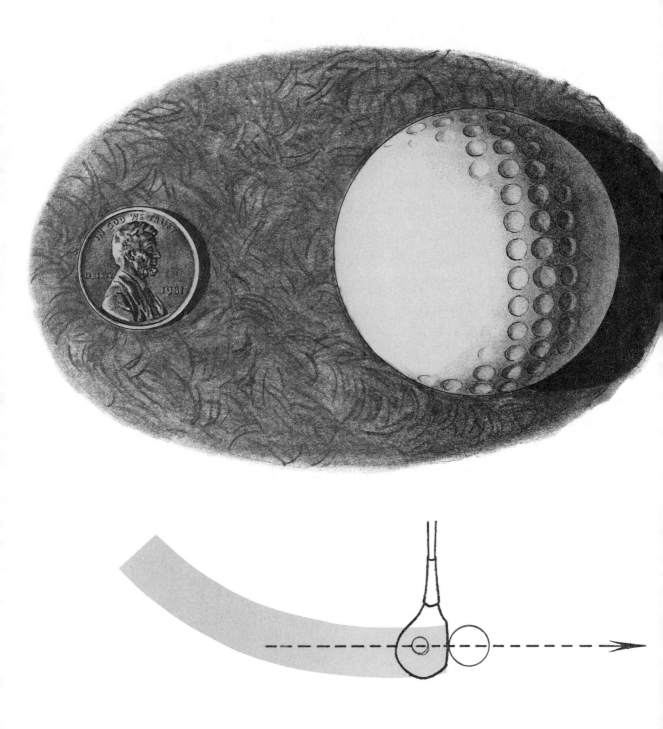

5

If you favor the 7-iron and your friends call you Alice when your name is Alex . . .

Swing at a coin behind the ball to increase club-head speed

If a "favorite club" poll were taken among golfers, I suspect that the 7-iron would rank quite high.

Why? Because this club is especially forgiving for that all-too-vast group of players who happen to create a certain set of impact factors on most of their shots. These impact conditions are:

• A clubhead path that is moving from outside to in-

51

side the target line, or toward left of target.

• An angle of approach that is too steeply downward, a common condition when the path is out to in.

• A clubface alignment that is "open," facing to the right of the path. Such facing is very common given the out-to-in path and the ultra-steep angle of approach.

On long shots, played with lesser-lofted woods and long irons, these impact conditions create unfortunate shots. The ball starts out to the left, that being the clubhead's path, and then slices to the right, because of the clubface being open to its path.

Topped shots to the left—again toward where the clubhead is moving—are also common to this pattern of impact. Teed shots are sometimes undercut upward because of the club's steep angle of approach.

Shots with more-lofted clubs, particularly the wedges, also tend to start left because of the clubhead's path, but unlike the longer shots they do not slice back to the right, despite the open-faced contact. This is because the high degree of loft on these clubs applies tremendous backspin to the ball. This backspin overrides the slice spin that would otherwise create the curve to the right.

The 7-iron is favored by these golfers because its loft is such that the amount of backspin applied does not quite override the sidespin. Enough slice spin remains to bring the leftward-starting shot back to the target. Also, this club's loft is sufficient to create shots of decent height despite the steeply downward approach.

Golfers who combine these impact conditions also desire, and need, more distance. The out-to-in, open-faced contact creates a glancing blow that reduces length, as does the steeply downward approach that sends too much force into the ground rather than forward. Also, golfers who have an out-to-in and steep swing through impact generally fail to move the club freely with their arms throughout the whole swing. Instead they swing themselves, overworking their bodies, so that the club's speed becomes more akin to their slower-moving parts, such as the shoulders.

If your shots approximate the pattern just described, your problems might be due to the way you start your downswing. Instead of freely swinging the club down from the inside with your arms and hands, you might be clinging onto it with your hands while your legs, hips and shoulders unwind to the left. This forces the club to move outward, into position for the out-to-in and steeply downward blow, before it can start downward from the inside.

With the hands clinging and locked and the arms starting downward too late, neither can do their share in squaring the clubface by impact. Instead,

the club lags behind the legs and hips and arrives at the ball with the face still open to the clubhead's path.

The solution is to try to swing the club downward from the inside with the arms before the body can unwind. The path from the inside makes the club's angle of approach less downward and more forward, for added distance. It also allows the arms to square the clubface by impact.

It took John Jacobs, the excellent British teacher, only two or three minutes to show me how to do this. The scene was a driving range in Augusta, Ga., during the 1969 Masters.

He had watched me make only two or three shots before he was assured that my swing pattern was comparable, unfortunately, to that of the golfer just described.

Before my next attempt, he placed a sprig of grass two or three inches behind the ball I was set to strike.

Failure to swing the club freely with the hands and arms (top-left illustration) leads to open-faced contact and shots that curve to the right. Attempting to strike a coin or sprig of grass behind the ball (top-right) leads to swinging the club back to the ball from inside to along the target line and squaring the face to that line by impact.

"This time," he said, "just make sure you catch this grass behind the ball."

Surprisingly, I did not stick the club into the ground behind the ball as I'd expected to do. It caught the ball solidly, flew it farther than my norm and even in a slight draw pattern, which in my case—being lefthanded—is from left to right. This satisfying pattern continued on succeeding attempts, each made with a sprig of grass behind the ball being my anticipated point of contact.

Later John explained that my efforts to strike grass behind the ball had forced me to swing the club down from the inside with my arms and hands before my legs and shoulders could unwind and force it to the outside.

The feeling I began to experience was that of swinging the club down solely with my arms while my back was still turned to the target. It is a feeling that you, too, should experience and cultivate if, indeed, you have been overworking your hips and shoulders.

This is not to say that the legs and body do not have a role to play in the golf swing. For golfers who overwork these parts, however, a coin or a sprig of grass behind the ball can help recreate the correct feeling of the arms also doing their fair share.

Another quick and simple way to make your arms swing the club freely is described in the next chapter. It is explained there, rather than here, because the drill involved also serves a second purpose, that being to restore a sense of proper pace and rhythm to one's swing.

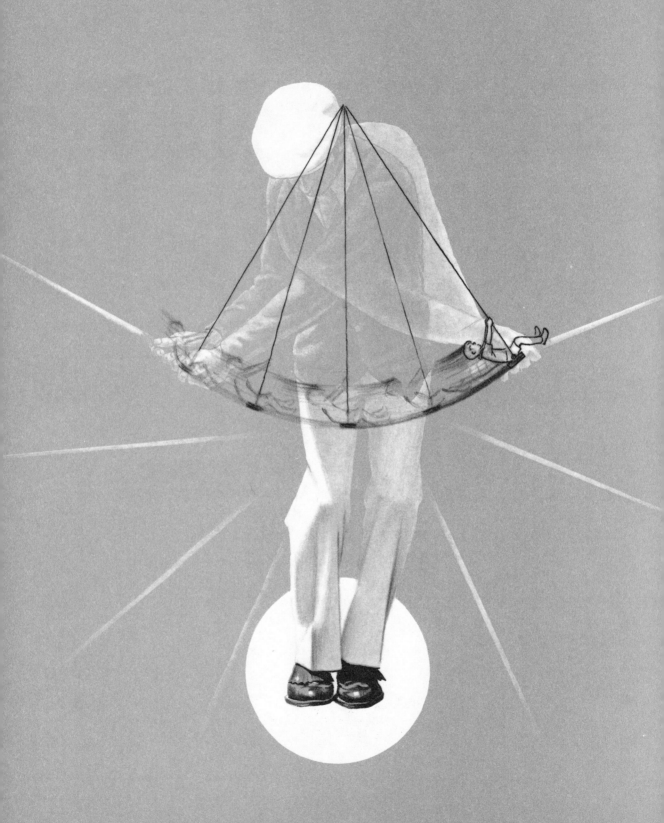

6

If swinging too hard makes you
lose your balance . . .

Put your feet together to improve your pace

Golfers who tend to overwork their shoulders often develop a pattern of contact that is like that of the players just described, those who tend to favor the 7-iron.

Overusing the upper body, as opposed to simply swinging the arms and letting the shoulders react, forces the clubhead to move steeply downward to the ball on an out-to-in path with the clubface remaining open during contact.

The results are long shots sliced from left to right, or sometimes topped to the left; drives often undercut weakly upward, and wedges and 9-iron shots pulled to the left of the flag, or flown toward the target but short.

Often these golfers also hold the club too tightly and swing too hard. Men who have played football extensively at a lineman's position, for instance, tend to swing in this shoulder-dominant manner.

The drill that follows, or some variation thereof, is often prescribed by Bob Toski, Jim Flick and John Jacobs, along with many other great teachers to be mentioned later. It is designed to force the arms to swing freely while the shoulders react passively. It is also an outstanding way to regain one's swing pace and rhythm.

All you must do is strike a few practice shots with your feet together, actually touching each other. For most players this works best with a 5-iron or 6-iron, and the ball resting on a low tee.

This drill works, as do so many, because it puts the golfer into a situation that forces his mind and body to react in certain correct ways.

With his feet together, he senses that his balance is in jeopardy, that his legs are not going to be of much help and that too much effort with his shoulders might send him sprawling. This leaves him largely dependent on his arms and hands to

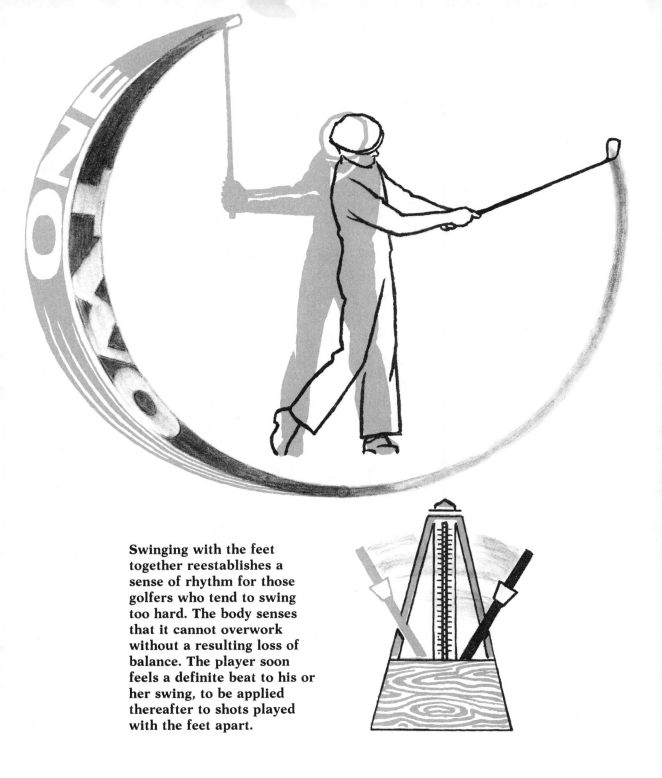

Swinging with the feet together reestablishes a sense of rhythm for those golfers who tend to swing too hard. The body senses that it cannot overwork without a resulting loss of balance. The player soon feels a definite beat to his or her swing, to be applied thereafter to shots played with the feet apart.

swing and square the club.

He also senses that swinging too hard or too fast might produce unfortunate results. Thus he reacts subconsciously by taking a bit more time to gather himself together between backswing and down-swing, just as a children's playground swing seems to pause between swinging up and starting down. His swing begins to take on a definite rhythm or beat. This usually happens within just four or five swings with the feet touching.

The overall result is an unhurried swinging of the arms. With the shoulders subordinated, the arms can swing the club back to the ball from inside to along the target line and then back to the inside, a path that encourages squaring the clubface as it moves through the impact area.

As is true for most drills, this one is meant to create correct feelings within the golfer that he can thereafter cultivate through practice. In this case the sensations to be identified, cherished and developed are those of the arms swinging on a pro-per path at a proper pace with the hands holding the club lightly throughout.

There will be a tendency to regress back to a harder, faster swing with undue grip pressure when you once again widen your stance. It is best to widen it gradually and only after your shots begin flying straight on target or hooking to the left. Return to the drill whenever the old left-to-right shape of shot reoccurs.

This drill can be applied during actual play on the course. Whenever your swing feels too fast or too hard, merely take a few practice swings with your feet touching before playing the shot. Then play it from a narrower than normal stance width.

Similar practice ploys that create the same results as swinging with the feet together include hitting shots barefooted or in slick-soled street shoes.

Peter Kostis

If you combine slicing with topping as you fire and fall back . . .

Find an upslope to improve your weight shift

Golf philosophers frequently draw comparisons between the game and life itself. Patience is a virtue. Hard work pays off. Trauma develops character. Success breeds success. The power of positive thinking. That sort of thing.

The teacher of golf sees another parallel, one that is fun to talk about even if it doesn't always hold true. At the risk of stereotyping, there is often a degree of tie-in between a pupil's job occupation and the way he or she responds to instruction.

For instance, doctors generally make excellent

students. They listen well, perhaps because listening to patients for diagnostic clues is an important part of their job. They tend to accept without remorse the bad shots that so often occur when changing from the old way to the new way—even a spurt of shanking cannot compare with losing a patient on the operating table. And they seem willing to commit themselves to a long-term program for improvement, perhaps because becoming a doctor requires a similar commitment.

Lawyers tend to question, if not dispute, the merit of the teacher's message. Doubting the instructor impedes their progress.

Some corporate executives lack the patience to persevere with changes over the long haul. They've learned to expect quick results from those they employ.

Conversely, golfers with a career in the military accept instruction well. What the pro requests is an order to be obeyed.

Salesmen are usually fun to teach, unless they show up with a hangover.

Among the more difficult students are those who make their living in exact sciences—accountants, mathematicians, engineers. Though well-meaning, they want to know everything about everything. They seek all available data. "Why did that shot slice?" "Do I need stiffer shafts in my woods?" "Is my backswing too short?" "Should I lift my left heel?" "When should my wrists uncock?"

The teacher who allows an answer to all questions is likely to produce a player who addresses the ball and swings by the numbers—far too many numbers. This type of player becomes frustrated, and thus still less effective, when all the numbers he's fed into the computer do not produce a shot that is slide-rule perfect.

One engineer who belies this stereotype, however, is Peter Kostis, a head instructor in the Golf Digest Instruction School program. Soon after earning his engineering degree, Peter decided it would be more fun to develop his own game and that of others than to build a rocket ship to Mars.

In the 10 or so years since, he has indeed succeeded on both counts. His playing skill borders on being of tour quality. His skill as a highly innovative, clear-thinking, communicative teacher is even greater.

And Peter is the only pro I know who's had a mountain named after him.

"Mt. Kostis" is an upward-slanted platform that Peter designed with typical engineering precision. It's for pupils who do not transfer their weight correctly. Those who strike shots up its slope quickly learn to shift from reverse to forward between backswing and downswing, through fear of falling off the mountain if they don't.

Practicing off an upslope that is similar in grade to Peter Kostis' "mountain" trains golfers to transfer weight correctly.

If you tend to topple off to your right on your follow-through, in which case many of your shots will be sliced or topped, it will help for you to similarly practice off an upslope. Find one that is not so steep that it totally disallows any weight transfer to the left. For most people a 15-degree slope is about right. This is one-sixth of the way from level to vertical.

Your end goal will be to shift weight from your right foot to your left foot at the start of your down-swing. This requires two things:

First, you must have something to shift, some weight on the right to be shifted to the left.

Second, you must allow enough time between backswing and downswing for the shifting to begin.

Thus the first feeling to notice and cultivate is that of more weight being on your right foot at address than is customary for you.

The inswing feeling to cultivate is that of pausing or gathering yourself together at the top of your backswing. Give yourself time to do a little down-ward and leftward pushing off from the inside of your right foot.

It will be best if at first you play these shots with a 5-iron or 6-iron, and with less than normal effort. Try to make the shots finish less than three-fourths of normal distance.

Your shots may tend to fly more to the left, or less to the right, than normal. This is due to the upslope; don't worry about it. Your only purpose is to develop the sensation of weight moving from right foot to left foot during your downswing, which will improve your shots in quick order once you return to level ground.

Periodic practice from the upslope will help insure that your tendency to fire and fall back does not reoccur.

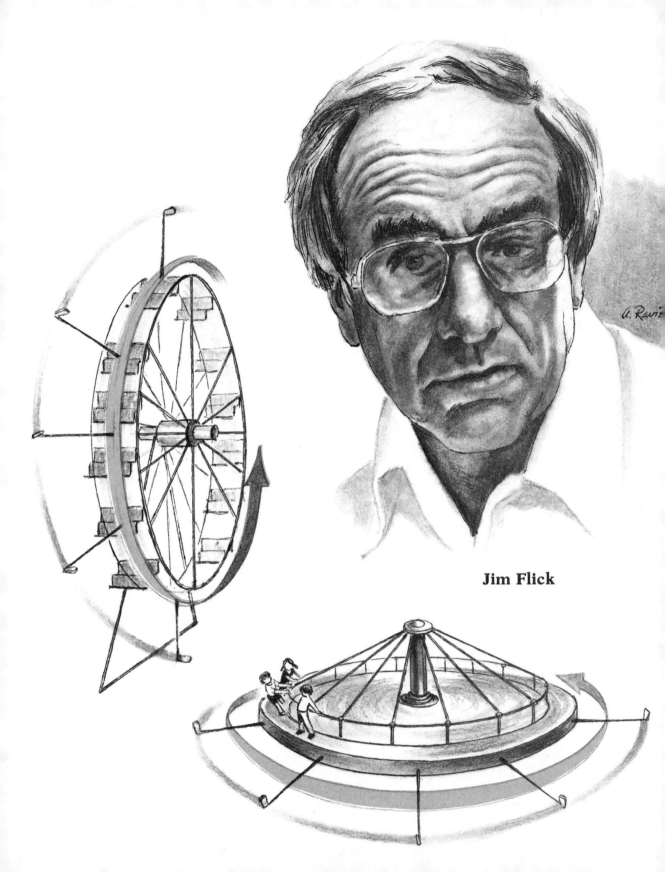

Jim Flick

If your shots fly too high or too
low, your swing may be too
upright or too flat . . .

Practice from sidehill slopes to change your swing plane

In the 1970 book, *The Square-to-Square Golf Swing*, Jim Flick and I presented the topic of swing plane in terms of a Ferris wheel and a merry-go-round. The Ferris wheel represented one extreme, the perfectly upright swing. The merry-go-round represented a perfectly flat swing.

Of course neither extreme is correct for golf. Because the ball sits on the ground, well below shoulder height, swinging like a merry-go-round would surely make the clubhead pass several feet above it. Swinging like a Ferris wheel is equally impractical, if not anatomically impossible, because we do stand to the side of the ball.

A useful swing plane is somewhere in between, but no single plane is ideal for every golfer. The ideal depends largely on the individual's physique and his posture and distance from the ball at address.

And no single swing plane will work for a given player on all of his or her shots. This is because our clubs vary in length and thus require that we stand varying distances from the ball. Normally you will swing flatter with a long club and more upright with a short iron.

Actually, there is usually more than one plane involved in a given swing. For instance, most good players swing the left arm on a slightly more upright plane than that on which their shoulders turn. This allows the arm to swing the club with more freedom and speed than might be possible if it were locked into the action with the slower-turning shoulders. Swinging the left arm on a bit more upright plane than the shoulders will not create good shots, however, if the shoulder-turn itself happens to be too upright.

Enough theory. Suffice it to say that you will want to turn your shoulders and swing the left arm on planes that let your clubhead find the ball squarely while moving in the right direction.

You probably will not know what your current swing planes are. However, as always, the pattern of your shots is your best diagnostic clue. It can indicate if your swing is too much up and down like the Ferris wheel or too much around like the merry-go-round.

If your swing is generally too upright, you will tend to hit some unusually high shots. Your long shots will tend to curve to the right because the ultra-upright swing discourages a free and natural turning of the club to the left with the hands and arms during the downswing.

Also, you may combine sticking the club in the ground behind the ball with lifting up and topping it. In the latter instances, you will feel to have "looked up." However, trying to keep your head down will probably make your swing more upright and thus increase your problems.

If your swing is generally too flat, your shots will tend to fly too low. You may be troubled by hooking, because the flat swing encourages too much turning of the club to the left during the downswing. You may have trouble pinching your iron shots—creating a somewhat descending blow—unless you've adjusted by playing the ball well back to the right of your hands. In that case you may tend to push your short-iron approaches to the right of target. Generally, you will probably prefer to play "winter rules."

75

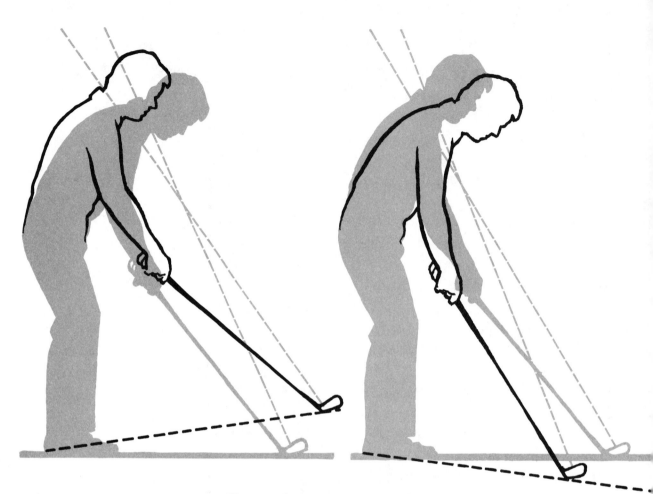

Golfers with swings that are too upright should practice on slopes with the ball above the feet (dashed lines at left). Those who need a less flat, more upright swing should practice from a slope with the ball below the feet.

If either of these shotmaking patterns sounds all too familiar, it would be worth your while to at least experiment with practicing off a gentle sidehill slope.

If your shot pattern indicates a too-upright swing, find a slope where you can play shots with the ball somewhat above your feet.

At first you will probably dislodge a goodly portion of hillside, because your swing will still be too up and down, and because the ball will be "higher" than normal in relation to your feet.

To adjust, first make sure that your chin isn't tucked down towards your chest at address. Lift it slightly before swinging. Also, choke down on the club an inch or two and try to swing it more around yourself instead of so much up and down.

If your shot pattern indicates that your swing may be too flat, practice off a sidehill lie with the ball slightly below your feet. At first you may top it. Bend slightly more forward from your hips—not your knees—and swing your arms more up and down, less around.

Sidehill practice is designed not only to force you to make a less upright or less flat swing, according to your needs, but also to *feel* the change. Once you begin to make solid contact off the slope, start to assimilate how your address position and swing feel, so that you can recapture those feelings on shots from level ground.

Do not be dismayed if your shots from the hillside tend to fly away from it, to the left if the ball is above your feet or to the right if it's below. This merely indicates that the experiment is working. The slope is forcing you to make changes that will lead to straighter shots in just a few tries once you return to level ground. And, most importantly, it is forcing these changes to happen naturally, without your having to make this or that part move in this or that way.

Bobby Jones

9

If you freeze over the ball like a
statue, you could turn into a
monumental failure . . .

Swing free with 'one-two-three'

In his excellent autobiography
Golf is My Game, published in 1959, the immortal
Bobby Jones politely questioned a certain trend
among the younger touring professionals of that
time.

"If there is a new method in golf," he wrote, "it
seems to involve a more careful, even meticulous,
'sighting' of the shot. While we still have many
graceful, comfortable-looking players, there are a
number who have the appearance of being excruciat-
ingly stiff.

"In some cases the traditional waggle of the club,
designed to promote smoothness of movement, has

been replaced by a waggle of the player's behind as he strives to place himself in precise position for the delivery of the blow."

"Some of these players are very effective," Jones added, "but the method involves a total disregard to the amount of time consumed, and so is most trying upon the nerves and patience of any who may be watching."

Were Jones still alive, he would notice that by now many golfers at all levels have discarded not only waggling the club, but the "behind" as well. For some, starting the swing seems to first require a mental summoning forth of a dozen or so instructional points, all of which require satisfactory checking off before the player dare activate a single muscle.

Standing over the ball too long, like a statue, can turn you into a monumental failure. Thinking too much while moving too little, lets mental and physical paralysis set in. Freedom of movement lessens. The backswing gets too fast, too jerky and often too short.

Jones, who was admired for his long, graceful, fluid swing, was a one-waggle man.

"Although we are in the habit of thinking of addressing the ball as one thing, and of swinging the club as quite another," he wrote, "it is a great aid to relaxation if the two performances can be blended as intimately as possible.

"Whenever I hesitated or took a second waggle, I could look for trouble."

The tendency to erect themselves alongside the ball is especially common among learning golfers, who often do have a number of things to keep in mind. More than once I have heard John Jacobs advise a pupil in such a state that "it seems to be getting dark."

Once I was out on the course with a group of pupils who had just gone through three days of intensive swing instruction. Typically, each was spending an inordinate amount of time preparing to swing. The checklists were long indeed.

But one woman in particular—we'll call her Mary—seemed to have more on her mind than anyone else. When it came her turn to shoot, she began what seemed to be a never-ending, immobile vigil over the ball, staring at it intently with head bowed forward.

As time passed, I could sense the tension building within the group. The other pupils began looking at each other in wonder. What could be wrong? Will she *ever* pull the trigger?

Finally, to break the grim silence, I asked the woman what seemed to be an obvious question:

"Mary, could it be that perhaps you are praying?"

In similar situations, I have seen Davis Love, an outstanding on-course instructor, advise the group beforehand that everyone would get only five counts before starting the club away from the ball. Then he counts aloud, "one, two, three . . .," starting as soon as the player sets the clubhead behind the ball.

This does throw some players a bit off-stride at first. Soon, however, they adjust and begin to put their thoughts in order *before* they move up to the ball, which is always a better policy.

Yes, Jack Nicklaus does spend considerable time at address. It is his nature. However, he has done this throughout his golfing life, not only on the course but also while striking a million or so practice balls. The time and thought that he has put into each practice shot has made doing the same thing on the course seem as natural to him as pulling the trigger quickly would be to a Jones, Trevino, Casper or Boros.

Whereas Jack practices as he plays, most amateur golfers spend more tension-producing time over the ball when on the course than they do on the range. This change of tactic adds to their uneasiness because it is, in itself, a different way of doing things. It is just one more reason why golfers seldom strike the ball as well during actual play as they do during practice.

Moreover, Nicklaus does something fairly unique at address that improves his chances of swinging freely thereafter. Instead of setting the clubhead on the turf, he holds it slightly above ground. From there he can swing it away smoothly without having to tighten his hands and arms in the slightest to dislodge it from the grass.

This is a technique long advocated by Eddie Merrins, head professional at Bel-Air Country Club in Los Angeles. I feel it can benefit any player who is willing to spend a practice session or two adapting to the change. As Eddie points out, "If your goal is to strike the ball, there is no point in addressing the ground behind it."

If you feel that your swing is too tight, too fast or too short, I suggest you try what I call the "one-two-three drill." It is designed to drastically shorten the time spent over the ball and thereby reduce tension. It will also create a definite rhythm or beat for your swing.

Applying the drill does require that you plan the shot before you move into your address position. You should have your target in mind, and you should "see" the path in front of the ball on which you want the shot to start.

Also, you should be holding the club lightly with little or no tension in your arms. The arms should feel soft and flexible, like two strings of cooked spaghetti.

Now, the drill itself:

1. After sighting down your target line, approach

85

the ball, set your right foot *only* into position and aim the club down your target line.

2. Swing your left foot into position so that your weight shifts onto it and toward your target. You may also feel yourself leaning in that direction after planting the foot. Fine.

3. Swing the club back with your arms as your

The one-two-three drill eliminates tension at address and creates proper weight shifting to the right during the back-swing.

weight rebounds from off your left foot and back on-to your right foot.

Though I've broken this down into three steps, your goal should be to make it all one continuous motion. Right foot, left foot, right foot. One, two, three.

Do it a few times with an imaginary ball until you begin to feel the beat. Then, initially, play the ball from a low tee.

Hold the club lightly at all times, all the way through impact.

You will probably mis-hit your first few shots, largely because you will not, as yet, have found ex-actly where to place your feet in relation to the ball. But stick with it. Do be as precise as you can in plac-ing your right foot and aiming the club down your target line.

Do not be disturbed if you feel yourself swaying, to the left as you place the left foot in Step 2, and then to the right as you rebound into your back-swing.

This is merely a drill but, hopefully, with practice, you will take much of it—perhaps all of it—into your actual shotmaking on the course. Short of that, it is still an excellent way to make your practice swings on the course, so as to experience beforehand the rhythm you'd like to feel when you play the upcom-ing shot.

Short Game Shortcuts

Jerry Pate

10

If your pitch and run-up shots
are letting you down . . .

Expand your arsenal, pick your best weapon

Jerry Pate is the first man in the last 20 years to win both the U.S. Amateur and Open championships. Recently we talked about a big difference that he sees between the touring pro and the so-called average golfer, in the way they handle their short shots to the green.

"Many amateurs will rely on their one favorite shot just about every time," he said. "They'll choose the same club, regardless of the conditions. They'll play the ball about the same place in their stance every time. They'll set themselves up to it the same way. The only thing that changes is the length or speed of their swing, depending on how far they want the ball to go."

Jerry went on to point out that the touring pro has literally hundreds of variations to choose from on these same shots. He might select any one of several clubs. He might play the ball forward or back in his stance to varying degrees. He might alter the width of his stance, or the alignment of his feet and body, or the extent that he grips down on the club. He might lay the blade back or hood it forward at address, or set it opened to the right or slightly closed to the left. He might pinch the shot low and running, or lob it high and soft. He might swing the club on a normal path, or he might cut the shot with an out-to-in path.

In most instances, the expert will make these variations with little or no conscious thought. His mind and body sense what modifications will create the particular type of shot that will most likely succeed in that particular situation.

There are times when the shot situation is so unusual that the expert must consciously manufacture a shot he's never played before. Even then, however, he will have made shots in the past that were somewhat similar, and therefore he will usually do quite well.

Jerry's main point is that the expert chooses from countless options the one that best fits the particular situation he faces. The less-skilled, less-experienced amateur has all too few options with which to face a countless variety of situations.

There is no easy way to become a Jerry Pate around the greens; it takes more than a few swings. In that respect, the top of building an overall short game does not really fit into the scope of this book.

I will discuss the topic in this chapter, however, because I do feel that there are four things you can do. They will not only expand your arsenal of options in relatively little time, but also will give you better results, *immediately*, through better use of whatever talents you now have.

I should add that, for most golfers, there is no quicker and surer way to lower their scores than through improving on short shots to the green.

For example, a typical golfer in the 15-25 handicap range will average at least 3½ shots to hole out from less than full-swing range of the green. He will be in this range at least 12 times on average per round. If he can reduce the 3½-stroke average to three—on the green and two putts—he will thus cut his overall score by six shots. The score-reducing potential is even greater for players with higher handicaps, who have even more room for improvement.

To improve your short approaches, there are four things to do, if you have not done them already:

1. Expand your arsenal. Practice short shots with three clubs, the 6-iron, 8-iron and pitching wedge. Learn how the ball reacts from each club—how high and far it flies and how far it rolls after landing on the green. Always watch your shots all the way to the finish.

Then do the same, but with the ball an inch or so farther back to the right in your stance. Do not, however, start with your hands or your weight setting any farther back to the right.

This simple adjustment will, in effect, turn the 6-iron into a 5-iron or 4-iron, the 8-iron into a 7-iron and the wedge into a 9-iron, thus further expanding your arsenal.

Eager players might also include the sand wedge in their arsenal. Its extra loft and sole weight create higher shots than you would normally get with the pitching wedge.

2. Learn to play each shot in a way that assures making contact while the club is still moving somewhat downward, before it reaches the bottom of its arc. (This is such a vital aspect of the short game that Chapter 12 in its entirety will deal with shortcuts for achieving such contact.)

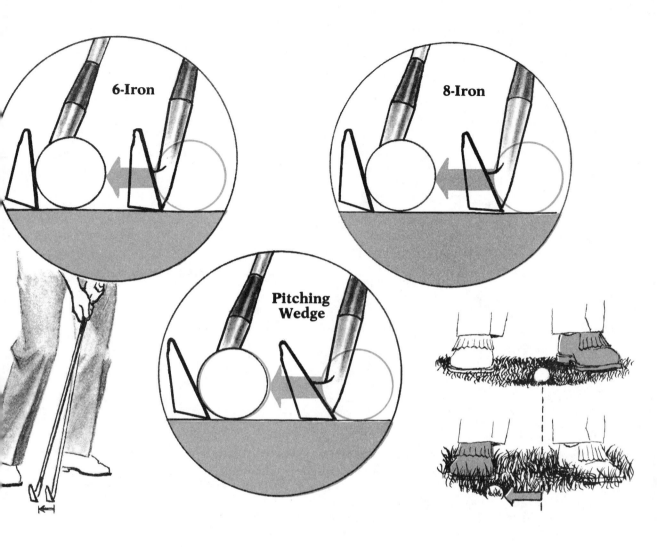

Serious golfers should learn to play short approach shots with at least three clubs. The 6-iron, 8-iron and pitching wedge are recommended. Each can be reduced in loft, to create the lower trajectory of a 5-iron, 7-iron and 9-iron respectively, by merely playing the ball a bit farther back to the right in the stance, as is mandatory for solid contact when the ball rests in a bad lie.

95

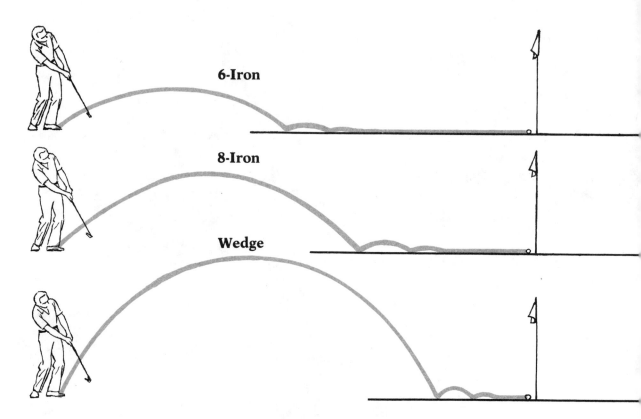

6-Iron

8-Iron

Wedge

Landing the ball safely on the green with minimum air time
with a 6-iron, 8-iron and wedge. In each instance the golfer
has chosen the club of minimum loft that allows landing just
on the green yet stopping in time. As the distance to the
green increases and/or the amount of green to the hole
decreases, the need for more loft increases.

3. Memorize this guideline:

Land the ball safely on the green, with minimum air time, whenever you can do so without its running well past the hole.

Please study this statement, and the explanation that follows.

Landing the ball "safely" on the green means landing it far enough beyond the fringe to avoid possibly landing short in the longer, rougher grasses that could thwart a true bounce.

"With minimum air time" means landing the ball no farther onto the green than is necessary to avoid landing short of it.

In other words, whenever you can do so without the ball running well past the hole, plan to land the ball safely beyond the fringe, but no farther onto the green than that.

For example, do not try to fly the ball up to near the hole with your wedge when you can land it just safely on the green and let it run up to the hole with your 8-iron. And do not do this with your 8-iron if you can do it with your 6-iron.

Put another way, always use the least-lofted club that will land the ball safely on the green without its running too far. Never use more loft than you need. This merely decreases your chances of making solid contact. The less the loft, the better the contact, as a general rule.

There will be situations, of course, where landing the ball just safely on the green is not feasible, where even a high shot with the wedge to a spot just beyond the fringe would not stop in time. Then you must discard this guideline and plan a shot that will land short of the green and bounce and roll up to the hole.

There will also be times when landing the ball safely on the green with minimum air time would require it to land on a sharp slope that could thwart its bounce. In that situation you must choose the lesser of three evils: (a) going ahead and taking your chances with landing on the slope, (b) landing short of the slope and risk landing short of the green or (c) landing beyond the slope with a higher shot, which would require using a more lofted—and thus riskier—club.

4. Always consider your lie.

Players who have trouble making these shots go the right distance usually fail because their contact with the ball is so inconsistent. And one reason it is so inconsistent is because they fail to allow for the lie of the ball in the grass.

A good rule of thumb to follow is this:

The worse the ball's lie is—whether it be deep in the grass or setting on a bare spot—the farther back to the right in your stance you should play it.

The purpose of playing the ball back is to assure contacting it with the club before the club catches in grass or turf behind the ball.

However, playing the ball back does make it fly lower than normal. Therefore, if the lie requires playing the ball back, you will need to select a more lofted club than you would otherwise have chosen.

A. Ravielli

11

If your lob shots to the green
tend to resemble small-arms
fire . . .

Float your wedges with full swing at part speed

If you were to attend a typical Golf Digest Instruction School, you would find yourself with 39 other students learning all phases of the game over a five-day period.

You would go to some 20-25 presentations by the teachers. You would receive individual tuition a total of 40-60 times from five or six different instructors. You would probably strike 2,500 or so shots, not including putts.

These schools have been tremendously successful,

growing from 17 students in 1971 to over 1,500 in 1980. But they do present a paradox.

On one hand Golf Digest feels obligated to provide a total curriculum. On the other, we all know that a given pupil can only absorb so much information and direction before he or she begins to self-destruct. How can these schools succeed when the regimen would seem to all but guarantee an epidemic of paralysis from over-analysis?

The solution lies partly in the fact that a golfer tends to display the same traits throughout all parts of his game. The player who cuts his putts, with the putterhead moving across his line to the left with the blade open to the right of that path, will usually do the same on his full shots. The player with a flippy full swing will usually be too wristy throughout his short game as well. The player who inadvertently aims his club to the right on full shots usually aims to the right when pitching, chipping and putting.

The tendency for a player to err the same ways on all shots allows the various instructors, who are teaching different shots, to provide him with a consistent improvement program. The needs of Pupil A might be entirely different from those of Pupil B, but the instruction that each receives from his putting teacher, his pitching teacher and his full-swing teachers will be consistent with his particular needs.

As a result, the effort that the pupil puts into improving his contact on putts and pitch shots will also help improve his impact on full shots, and vice versa.

Still, it would not be possible for the various teachers to provide a unified instruction program for each student if they themselves were not closely attuned to each other's methods. To avoid confusing a student, each teacher must be able to explain just how his particular piece of advice complements that of another instructor.

The teachers do understand each other's ways, and they continue to improve as teachers by learning from each other. Almost every week a teacher will discover some new and successful way to solve a problem or to motivate a pupil. Then he will pass it along to his fellow-teachers.

Sometimes we learn from watching each other. One day at a school in Boca Raton, Fla., in 1979, I happened to return early from lunch and found that Bob Toski was demonstrating a particular wedge shot for a small group of students and teachers.

He was playing from just a few yards off the practice green, but the green itself was raised and the target hole was just a few paces onto the putting surface.

His shots were flying unusually high and soft for such a short distance. The ball seemed to all but hang in mid air before it plopped down near the hole, like a butterfly with sore feet.

Bob was making what appeared to be unusually

103

long swings for such a short shot. His arms were swinging almost fully back and up on the backswing. And he was completing each swing with what looked to be a full follow-through, with his weight all but completely shifted onto his left foot.

The reason his shots were not flying far over the green was because he was swinging so slowly, at less than even half his normal speed. And, typically for Bob, he was obviously holding the club lightly, barely caressing the grip.

Early that afternoon I taught pitching to a group of 10 players, each with a handicap of over 20. The approach I used—and still use—stemmed directly from having watched Bob during the lunch break. Within just a few minutes, every member of that group was pitching their shots to the green exceptionally well almost every time.

What I did with that group might help improve not only your pitch shots, but also your sand shots and full shots from grass, if you will apply to them what you will be forced to feel when pitching.

The drill will be especially helpful if you happen to be a player who swings with too much fervor on your full shots, in which case you may have noticed that you tire rather quickly during your practice sessions.

You are also a candidate for this drill if you tend to combine skulling or topping the ball with hitting behind it on your short approach shots, in which case you are probably inconsistent on shots from greenside bunkers as well.

For this drill you will need a wedge—sand or pitching—and a bucket of practice balls.

First, decide how far you would normally fly the ball with this club on a good shot with a full swing. Then station yourself about one-half to three-fourths of that distance from a target, be it a practice green or merely a spot down the range. Be sure to find a nice area of grass from which to play.

Then, without the club in your hand, assume your normal address posture, bending forward from the hips, with your arms hanging loosely down in front of you.

Next, start swinging your arms continuously back and forth. Gradually lengthen their motion until you are making full swings both back and forward. Let your body turn and your weight shift in response to your arms swinging.

Force yourself to make a full finish each time, as shown in the illustration on page 100. Particularly, finish as shown with your weight shifted almost entirely onto the outside of your left foot, and with only the toe of your right foot touching the ground.

To reach this position, you will first need to complete your backswing.

Avoid finishing the swing with your head still

"down." And avoid sliding it to the left, as shown, during your follow-through.

For many readers, finishing the swing as shown here will feel different, more complete, than normal.

Each time you do swing to this full-finish position, identify just how you feel, especially in your feet.

Next, with club in hand, make a few more full practice swings. Before each swing, try to sense how you should feel at the finish. Then, after a full backswing, try to finish that way.

Continue doing this until you can finish fully, again as shown here, but without losing your balance.

Finally, strike balls to your target. Each time swing fully, all the way back and then all the way to the same full finish you've been making.

Your first few shots may go too far, but continue swinging fully. Soon your shots will continue to fly high, but not so far. They will start to land softly near your target.

When this happens, think about how your swing feels. It should feel full but considerably slower than normal. And your grip should feel extremely light from start to finish.

If things go bad for a spell, it probably will be

Golfers dramatically improve their pitch shots by making full swings at less than full speed to a target that is less than full-shot distance away. The shots fly progressively shorter, higher and softer as the player gradually increases the duration of his swing.

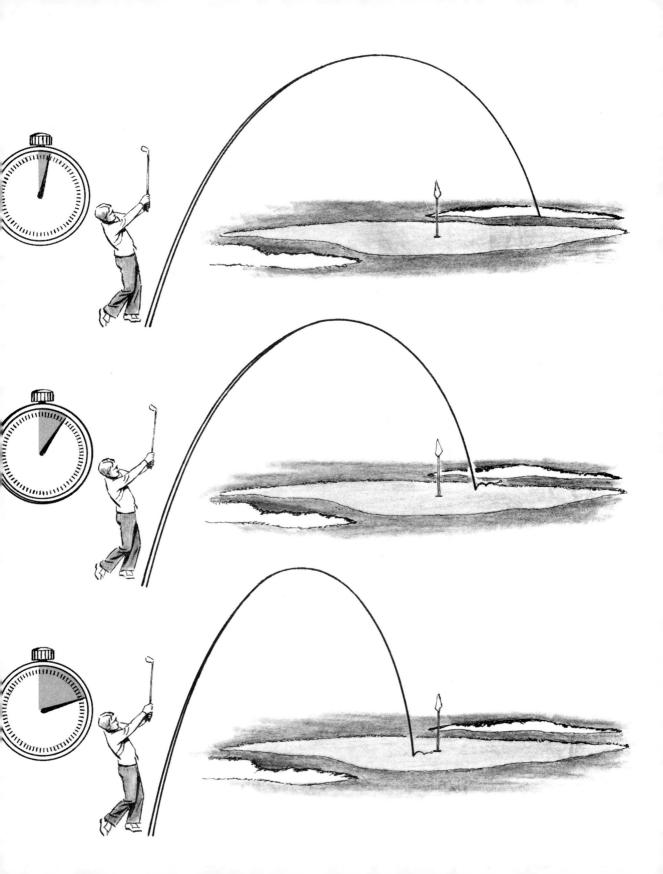

because you have forgotten to make a full swing both back and forward. Again, focus before you swing on how you want to finish. Sense how your feet should feel. Swing to that position, with a light grip all the way.

This weight transfer is especially important on these shots, where the normal urge is to flip the club underneath the ball with the right hand, a tendency that either flips it down into the ground behind the ball or upward into its backside.

To avoid this happening, your left arm and hand must nose out the clubhead in the race back to the ball. It is the weight transfer to the left during the downswing that helps them accomplish this mission.

This drill will, in itself, create high, soft pitch shots. However, it is also a drill to use, to the letter, for your normal sand shots from greenside bunkers. It applies on these shots as well because in sand the unfortunate urge to flip the ball up and out is even stronger, and because the loose footing tends to stifle shifting your weight into a full finish.

The drill will also help improve your rhythm, pace and balance on full shots from grass with the other clubs, as well as your tee shots, so long as you continue to hold the club lightly from start to finish.

To play shorter pitch shots and chip shots, you will need a shorter backswing and a lower finish with the hands. But do continue to hold the club lightly throughout, so that shortening the swing does not make it faster. And do continue to do at least some shifting of weight to the left during your downswing, even on chip shots from just off the fringe.

Al Geiberger

If you seldom take turf in front
of the ball, then what you need
are . . .

Six ways to pinch your approach shots

There is a Jekyll-Hyde transformation that overcomes some golfers during that brief period between the practice swing and the swing that counts.

A gentleman named Ike Handy once wrote a whole book about this phenomenon. He titled this book, quite aptly, *It's the Damn Ball.*

It is, indeed, the ball that triggers the change, from first making an effortless, unconscious swishing of the club at nothing in particular to then attempting an all-too-specific task with full effort and intense concentration.

It is the ball that makes us TRY. And it is the trying that so often does us in.

Most golfers make wonderful swings when knocking off dandelions, but only because it matters not whether the dandelion flies into the air, travels in a certain direction, goes a goodly distance. These things matter only when the ball is involved, when we must try to make them happen.

It is only natural that when we try to do something, we fall back on ways that have worked in the past, when we've tried to make something go high or straight or far. But we often fail in golf because the things that worked so marvelously well in other aspects of living do not apply. The things that seem so logical and feel so comfortable are, with club in hand, sometimes altogether wrong.

This is especially true on short shots to the green, those that require a swing that is less than full.

We all know that these shots are supposed to go into the air. Even a run-up shot with a 6-iron should fly upward and forward to some extent.

And everything we have done in life has taught us that making something go up requires our getting under it and then making some sort of upward movement. To lob a tennis ball high, we swing the racket upward. To throw a baseball high, we swing our arm upward. The same under and upward movement applies to volleyball, handball, shoveling snow, digging

112

"Dr. Jekyll"   "Mr. Hyde"

out weeds, scooping a spoonful of sugar, and so on. Under and up is the natural movement.

Thus it is natural that golfers swing the club slightly upward to the ball on these short shots to the green.

Unfortunately, swinging it upward actually makes the ball go too low most of the time. The leading edge of the blade cuts into the back side of the ball and skulls it across the green, low and hot.

When the golfer sees these shots flying too low, he naturally swings the club even more upward to the ball on succeeding tries. And the ball flies still lower more of the time.

Sometimes, when he makes the under-and-upward movement, his club snags in the turf behind the ball before continuing upward into it. Then his first thought is that he has swung the club too much *downward*. Why else would it dig in behind the ball?

Again, his natural reaction is to swing more upward thereafter.

The urge to swing upward seems to increase with the loft of the club in hand. The extreme upward facing of the wedge, for instance, seems to tell the player that this club is *supposed* to make the ball fly exceptionally high. So he swings it more upward into the ball than he would, say, the less-lofted 6-iron. That same player might not swing upward at all with the putter or the driver, the two clubs in his bag with the least amounts of upward facing.

The urge to help the ball up also increases when the ball rests down deep in the grass or on barren ground. Then the ball seems to cry for extra help from the player to get it out and up.

By now you may have guessed, correctly, that consistent success on these shots requires that the club be moving at least somewhat *downward* at contact, so that it grazes or pinches the back of the ball. It is true that the expert player might lob the ball into the air with a level-moving clubhead when the ball sets up high on the grass. For the average golfer, however, the level angle of approach is too close to being an upward approach to be a safe bet. And even the expert will invariably create a somewhat downward approach if the ball's lie is less than perfect.

At this time it would be well for you to decide whether you do, in fact, need to improve your ability to create a descending blow, and thereby improve not only your short approach shots, but also all iron shots played off the grass.

Here are some shot patterns that would indicate this need:

● If your short approach shots often fly too low and you seldom remove any grass, even on fairly decent shots. Or, if you fit this pattern but sometimes scrape turf behind the ball as well.

● If you seldom take a divot *in front* of the ball's position on your full shots with the 6-, 7-, 8- and 9-iron and pitching wedge. (In which case you probably refrain from using the sand wedge off grass.)

● If on sand shots from around the greens you often pick the ball too cleanly and fly it too far, or if you vary between taking too little and too much sand. (In which case you may have decided it's best to chip the ball out, rather than take a full swing.)

● If you are bothered on short approach shots when the ball is nestled down in the grass. (In which case you much prefer playing "winter rules.")

If these patterns apply to you, then there are certain general concepts you should understand before taking corrective steps:

● Your clubs already carry enough built-in loft to make the ball fly a normal height. There is no need for you to help it upward.

● Your shots will actually fly higher when the blow is slightly downward. The club's downward movement adds backspin to the ball, which helps it climb.

● The club's somewhat downward approach allows it to clear much of the grass and all of the turf behind the ball. Avoiding this interference is especially important on these short shots because the club is moving at a relatively slow speed anyway. The worse the lie of the ball—the greater the risk of such interference—the more downward the club's approach should be.

● Because the somewhat downward approach improves the quality of the contact, it helps assure that the ball will go the right distance. Good distance control is especially vital on these shots, where coming up too short or blading the ball too far is likely to cost you at least one full stroke.

● It is possible to drive the ball too low if the club is moving too steeply downward at contact, but even then the results are usually better than if the club were moving upward.

● To create a downward angle of approach, the left

hand and arm should lead the clubhead back to the ball. (Right hand and arm for left-handers.) They are not likely to lead the clubhead if the right hand flips it forward.

●Some shifting of weight to the left during the downswing, even on very short approach shots, helps the left hand and arm lead the clubhead back to the ball, thus creating a descending blow. For some players this shifting of weight to the left is not only helpful, but mandatory. Shifting weight to the left also helps the clubhead move downward to the ball itself, rather than into the ground behind it.

●Shifting some weight to the left during the downswing requires a leisurely swing pace. Swinging too fast gets the clubhead back to the ball before the shifting can take place.

●Playing the ball well back to the right in the stance helps insure that the left hand and arm will lead the clubhead into the striking area. It is usually better to err by playing the ball too far back than too far forward, so long as you resist the temptation to flip the clubhead underneath it.

●Holding the club with an extremely light grip pressure might well be the one thing most likely to improve your iron play, but only if you resist the tremendous temptation to go from light to tight during the swing. The idea of swinging the club downward to the ball, and then into the grass, tends to increase this temptation.

117

I wish I could assure you that merely understanding these concepts will guarantee your creating a descending blow on these shots. Unfortunately, for many golfers, the urge to somehow help the ball upward is so deeply ingrained that mere understanding—though helpful and often vital—is not enough.

These players must actually experience such contact. They must feel the solidity of contact and see the ball fly higher as a result, on shot after shot. Only then do they develop sufficient trust that the new way is better.

Because the descending contact is so important to your iron play, especially around the greens, I will now present several different situations that are designed to force you to create and experience it. I will leave it up to you to pick the one that works best for you.

Again, once your shots do improve as a result of performing within the forced situation you happen to choose, begin to identify how your address position and swing feel, so that you can repeat these feelings under normal conditions.

Also, before you try any of these drills, I recommend that you re-study and absorb the general concepts that I have just presented.

Turn your feet to the left
This drill, advocated by Al Geiberger, 1966 PGA champion, will help you shift some weight to the left

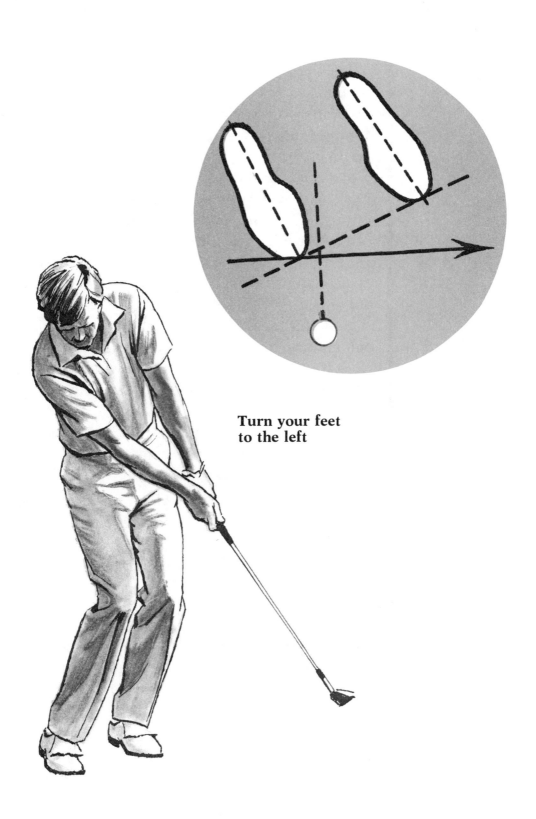

**Turn your feet
to the left**

during the downswing on your short shots. Again, this will help your left hand and arm pull the club downward to the ball, rather than your right hand flipping it upward.

With an 8-iron or 9-iron in hand, but without a ball in place, set up to play an imaginary chip shot. Check the illustration to be sure that (a) your feet are no more than four or five inches apart, if that, (b) both feet are turned well to the left and (c) your left toe is pulled back an inch or two, so that a line across your toes would extend well to the left of your imaginary target.

From this position, start by making some short back and forth swings, as you would on a chip shot, but without stopping between swings. Swing the club freely and rhythmically, brushing the grass. Hold the club lightly.

Now, as you swing the club back and forth with your arms, let your knees begin to glide back and forward as well. Coordinate this knee-glide with your arm swing. Then try to pick up the feeling that your knee-glide is making your arms swing.

Finally, play some chip shots from this same stance and incorporating the knee-glide.

Again, hold the club lightly.

Swing the club *through* the ball's position with your arms and knees; don't be concerned about striking the ball precisely.

If you find that you are brushing the grass behind

the ball, merely play it farther back to the right in your stance.

Once you begin to make solid contact consistently, do the same drill with your wedge and, thereafter, on gradually longer pitch shots.

Continue to play your short approach shots from this same stance, even during your rounds on the course.

Swing with only left hand on the club

Adopt the same stance as prescribed in the preceding drill, but hold the club only in your left hand.

Make some back and forth swings, without a ball, as described in that drill. Again, develop the feeling of your knees gliding to the left during your downswing.

Then, still without a ball, lighten your hold on the club. Swing it back and up with your left arm. Then, as your knees glide to the left, while still holding the club lightly, merely let it fall back to the ground of its own accord. Do not help it down or forward. Let gravity do the work.

Continue doing this until your clubhead drops into the turf time after time where the ball would normally be. Just let the club dig out a nice little chunk from its falling down at this spot.

Finally, do the same with the ball in position. Just let the club fall back to the ball on its own as your

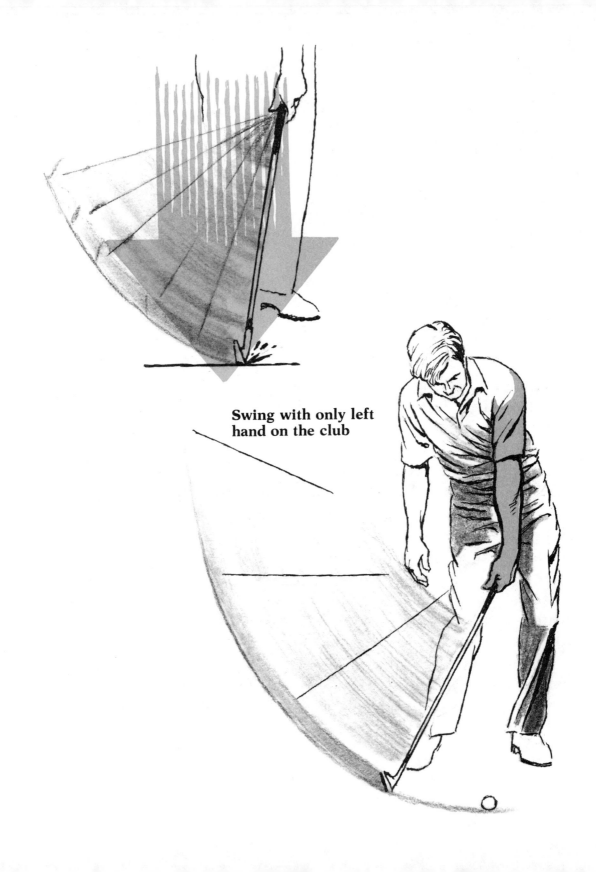

**Swing with only left
hand on the club**

knees glide to the left.

If you have trouble taking a divot, it will probably be because you are increasing your grip pressure as you swing.

If your club continually digs in behind the ball, merely play it back farther to the right in your stance, and be sure to give yourself enough time between backswing and downswing to start your knee-glide to the left.

Continue playing these shots until your club consistently catches the ball just before it enters the turf. Thereafter, put your right hand on the club—lightly. Continue making the same swings, but let your right hand come off the club just after contact.

Finally, keep your right hand on the club throughout the entire swing.

If you suddenly find your club is not taking a bit of turf in front of the ball's position, or at least brushing the grass there, it will be because you are (a) increasing your grip pressure before or during your swing and/or (b) swinging too fast.

Finish low

Play a few practice shots with your 9-iron or wedge to a target that is about 20 paces away. After each shot, notice where your clubhead is at the finish of your swing. Try to hold it in position, without letting it drop, until you have had a chance to look.

If you find that the clubhead finishes higher than

your shoulders on your bad shots, or even on the fairly decent shots that you happen to pick cleanly off the grass, you will know that this drill applies to your needs.

Thereafter, make several practice swings until the clubhead consistently finishes below *waist height. (See figure on page 119.) Do not* shorten your backswing to let this happen. And *do not* tighten your grip to curtail your follow-through. *Do* hold the club lightly and swing it rhythmically, just as if you were playing a shot of 20 paces.

Once you find that the club no longer finishes higher than your waist, you should begin to sense that it is moving more steeply downward toward where the ball would be.

Then apply this same practice stroke to your actual shots with the ball in position. Do not be concerned about contacting the ball precisely, however, or about how high it will fly. Merely hold the club lightly and then focus solely on making the clubhead finish as low as it did during your practice swings.

Strike an object in front of the ball

As you practice your short approach shots, before each try, place a small object, such as a penny, a match or a sprig of grass about two inches ahead of the ball.

Address the ball with the club as you normally do,

but focus on striking the object instead.

After just a few tries, you should find that your clubhead is actually striking the ball first and then the object, even though you are focusing only on the object as you swing.

If you find that you continually take turf behind the ball, or if you catch the ball thin without moving the object thereafter, you should play both the ball and the object a bit farther back to the right in your stance. Play them farther and farther back until you do, in fact, begin to create ball-then-turf contact.

If you find yourself topping the ball enroute to contacting the object, you probably will need a lighter grip pressure throughout your swing and a less aggressive downswing.

Position one ball behind the other

Practice short approach shots with your 9-iron or wedge. Before each shot place a second ball a short distance behind the ball you intend to play, to your right of it. This distance should be equal to the length of the grip on your club.

At first, set up to the ball you intend to strike and make a normal backswing. If your clubhead bumps the trailing ball during your takeaway, or if you feel that you've lifted the club to clear it, then you will need to adjust your feet. You will need to move more to your left so that, in effect, both balls are farther

125

back to the right. Continue adjusting in this direction until you can *swing* the clubhead freely back and up and over the trailing ball without feeling you have *lifted* it.

Once you find the positioning that allows a free backswing, go ahead and play the shot. Continue with this drill until you can consistently strike the original ball solidly without catching the trailing ball during your downswing.

Swing as freely as you can, with no sudden increase in your grip pressure as you do.

Point right finger behind the ball

An excellent drill for golfers who tend to flip the clubhead forward and upward with the right hand was taught to me by Dale Mead, head professional at Del Rio G. and C.C., Modesto, Calif.

Dale advises that, on short approach shots, the player first grip the club with his or her right forefinger extended down the trailing side of the shaft, just as some people extend this finger down the shaft when putting.

Thereafter the golfer's sole thought should be to contact the ball with this finger still pointing to a spot just behind the ball's position.

If you should find that this thought causes your club to top the ball while still moving downward, continue to employ the same thought but with a feeling of lightness in your hands, wrists and arms throughout your forward swing.

If you find that this thought improves your contact on short shots, it could also help your full shots, even your drives. Again, however, swing with the same feeling of lightness in your hands, wrists and arms that you felt on the short approach shots.

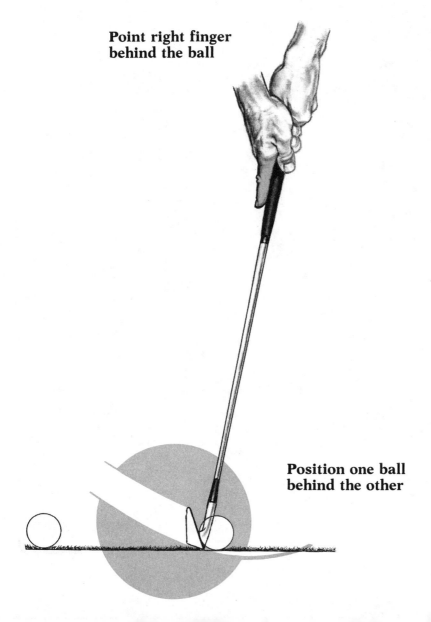

**Point right finger
behind the ball**

**Position one ball
behind the other**

13

If your first putts miss by 4 feet
and 4-footers give you palsy . . .

Build putting control by getting closer to your business

Golfers have been known to choke on four-foot putts with nothing more than a 50-cent Nassau bet on the line. At the other end of the spectrum there is Paul Trevillion, a British golfer who was willing to bet his life on sinking a putt of that length.

During the late 1960s and early 1970s, Trevillion's skill on such putts received considerable attention in the British press. It was said that he never missed, and that he would take on any challenger, pro or amateur, in a four-foot putt-out.

Trevillion, an artist by profession, wrote and illustrated articles explaining his technique. It featured holding the putter with hands well apart, the right hand far down the shaft. This grip allowed him to crouch and bend so far forward and downward that he could all but blow the ball into the hole.

It also led to his inventing and marketing a mini-length putter, one that let the player do all this crouching and bending without impaling his tummy with the top of the shaft.

To promote this putter in America, Trevillion approached Ken Bowden, then the editorial director of Golf Digest magazine who has since become a key figure in the Jack Nicklaus organization.

His proposal to Bowden was simple, and bizarre. After Ken had set up the promotion, Trevillion would walk out onto a platform that extended out from the top of the Empire State Building. He would attempt one putt—a four-footer—into a hole cut out of the platform.

If he missed, he'd jump.

Ken maintains that Trevillion was totally serious in making this proposal.

"It told him it was crazy," Bowden says. "No one would allow such a stunt. I even explained that if he did jump, he'd still land on a balcony partway down.

So then he talked about trying for the Brooklyn Bridge instead."

We'll never know if Trevillion would have made the putt, or jumped if he missed. I do know, however, that many golfers could improve their putting in just a few minutes by adopting one aspect of Trevillion's technique, by crouching down and bending forward from the hips so as to get, as short-game maestro Paul Runyan says, "closer to your business."

Take your putter and address a ball in front of a mirror. A full-length mirror would be ideal, but not mandatory.

Your first adjustment should be to crouch down and bend forward until a line across the back of your head and upper back would be horizontal, or parallel with the floor, as shown in the illustration on the next page. Check yourself in the mirror.

To help yourself find this horizontal position, feel free to move your hands farther down on the putter.

If you have been standing taller than this on your putts, this new position will feel terribly cramped and unnatural at first. So be it. Your image in the mirror will not look nearly so unnatural as you feel. In fact, you will resemble Nicklaus, Lee Trevino and all the other fine putters who assume a similar posture.

Positioning yourself in front of a mirror and dangling a putter from your nose are excellent ways to check putting posture and distance from the ball.

With the mirror as your guide, practice moving into this position until you can duplicate it every time.

Thereafter, check to see if your eyes are more or less over what would be the line of your putt. If not, merely move your feet closer to it or farther from it until your eyes hover above it. Be sure to move only your feet; do not bend farther forward or lean back, which would alter your posture.

To check your eyes' position if you lack a full-length mirror, or whenever you're putting outdoors, simply dangle the putter from your nose with your thumb and forefinger as shown in the illustration. Then the position of the putterhead will indicate if you need to stand closer or farther from the line.

Just be sure that you do not change your posture from the horizontal position when you lift the putter to your nose, or thereafter to get your eyes over the line.

If this positioning does bring you "closer to your business," you should discover that your contact on putts becomes more consistently solid after a few minutes' practice. Also, you will begin to sense that you have more control over the club and the direction and distance it rolls the ball.

If you are now gripping farther down the shaft, you may find that your early putts come up short. You will automatically compensate for this in a very short time. In fact, your control of distance should rapidly improve, even on longer putts of, say, 30-50 feet. This should happen because being closer to your business will help you contact the ball on the "sweet spot" of the putter more of the time. It is largely the alternating between hitting and missing this spot from putt to putt that causes one putt to run too far and the next to come up short.

I should warn against your practicing from this new address position in long stints. Quit or take a break if your back begins to stiffen or ache.

If this new address position helps your putting, there is no reason why you should not at least grip farther down on the club and stand closer to the ball on your chip shots from off the green as well.

Paul Runyan

If flipping your wrists is in-
flating your scores on mammoth
modern greens, it may be time to . . .

14

Make a wrist-free stroke with the putter against your arm

There is a certain parallel be-
tween the evolution of the species and the development of athletic technique. Darwin might have
found it interesting.

As he discovered, in the evolution of living
creatures, certain mutations crop up that better suit
their environment. Therefore, they thrive and multi-
ply and, eventually, become the norm.

Similarly, in sports, certain individuals come up

with a better way of coping with their environment—a better way of sprinting or jumping, say. These gifted athletes become the heroic models for those who are learning the sport. In time their unique way of performing becomes the standard way.

In basketball, for instance, Hank Luisetti's originally unique one-handed shooting style eventually led to the demise of the two-hand set shot. George Mikan spawned a generation of hook-shot artists. High-scorers like "Jumpin' Joe" Fulks showed youngsters how to leap before launching the ball. Schoolyard players also began to mimic Bob Cousy's behind-the-back passing and dribbling. And, finally, Julius Erving helped make the slam-dunk the ultimate test of basketball manhood.

Outstanding golfers, such as Vardon, Jones, Nelson, Snead, Hogan, Nicklaus and Watson, have similarly influenced apprentice players both young and old.

There is a bit of difference, however, between the things that stimulate "mutations" in basketball and in golf technique.

In basketball, the nature of the competition itself sparked the changes. The game has gone from slow and methodical, with a jump ball at center court after each basket, to a panorama of dazzling speed. Once it was played by men of normal stature; today even the *high school* All-American teams average over 6'-7".

Thus, in this sport, the lasting changes have been those that allowed moving the ball and triggering shots faster, and in ways that better avoided faster and taller defenders.

In golf the nature of the opposition has had far less to do with stimulating changes in technique. Far more influential, for instance, have been changes in the courses themselves.

Whereas the size of basketball courts and the height of the baskets have remained constant, golf course measurements have increased drastically. Today, the men's pro tour plays courses that average at least 400 yards longer than the average of 25 years ago. And these courses actually "play" additionally longer because of their added softness and lushness, created by the installation of fairway watering systems.

As courses have gotten longer and longer, greens have become bigger and bigger, and more densely surrounded by hazards of water and sand.

All of these changes have altered the players' priorities. Longer holes with softer fairways have created the need for additional carry on drives. At such courses as Augusta National, site of the Masters, a few more yards of flight off the tee, to reach a downhill landing area, can bring the player three or four clubs closer to the green, or give him a chance to safely carry over a hazard on his second shot to a green on a par-5 hole.

Lusher fairways demand a more-descending blow on iron shots to dislodge the low-lying ball solidly.

With the holes longer and with hazards now fronting many greens, there has developed a need for additional height and backspin on approach shots with the long irons—a need that many women professionals find especially difficult to meet.

These needs—more height, more carry, more backspin—have produced a trend to more upright swing planes, à la Jack Nicklaus and Tom Watson, more emphasis on leg drive, and more stress on pulling down and through with the left arm and hand in control.

Additional sand and water around greens has made the run-up shot a lesser part of golf, at least in America.

But the mammoth greens have made putting even more important. The best players of any generation have invariably been good putters, often outstanding. Today, however, it is all but impossible to even survive, especially on the men's tour, without an excellent putting technique and the willingness to maintain and improve it through countless hours of practice.

With this need to putt better has come a major change in technique, perhaps the most dramatic

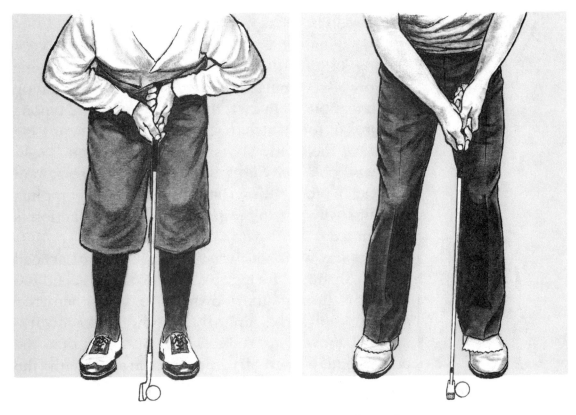

The evolution from wrist putting to arm putting has brought forth a major change in the address position. The old "elbows out" positioning, conducive to wristiness, has been replaced by more arm extension with the elbows closer in to the side, which is more likely to create free swinging of the arms.

we've seen in all aspects of playing the game.

This change has been from an arm and wrist stroke—often with more wrists than arms supplying the force—to a pure, wrist-free arm-stroke, even on the longer putts. In fact, there is even a trend among the pros of today also to apply the wrist-free putting stroke to their chip shots from off the green.

In his book, *The Short Way to Lower Scoring,* Paul Runyan, a pioneer of wristless putting and chipping, explains why putting improves when wrist action is eliminated:

"Flipping with the wrists makes the putterhead lift too abruptly during the backstroke, descend too abruptly during the downstroke and then flip abruptly upward again. All this upward-downward-upward movement reduces the duration that the putterhead is actually moving parallel with the ground at ball level. It also reduces the duration during which the club is carrying the proper amount of effective loft.

"It can reduce the duration during which your putterface is aligned square to its path.

"It can reduce the duration your putterhead is moving along the line you have chosen.

"Most certainly, any flipping of the wrists loosens your grip, thus reducing your control of the putter.

"Moreover, flipping the wrists also adds another speed-producing element to the stroke. . . . This added element makes it more difficult to control distance."

Changing to wrist-free putting may require that you first modify your hold on the club slightly. It will certainly require that your left arm pace the stroke through contact with the ball and beyond. If this arm stops or slows near contact, the right hand takes over and flips the putterhead forward and upward.

Regarding your grip, merely make sure that the putter extends upward along the lifeline of your left hand, in the channel between the thumb pad and heel pad (see illustrations on page 144).

If you have not already held the club this way, you should find that doing so tends to make your hands set higher. This higher positioning helps "freeze" your wrists *without* your needing to increase your grip pressure.

If this grip is new to you, it will feel a bit unnatural at first, but less so after a few minutes of practice.

Following such practice, here is the drill you should perform to assure that you do, in fact, pace your forward stroke with your left arm and thus disallow any wrist play:

Grip the putter as described and then slide your hand down the shaft until you can rest the top of it

143

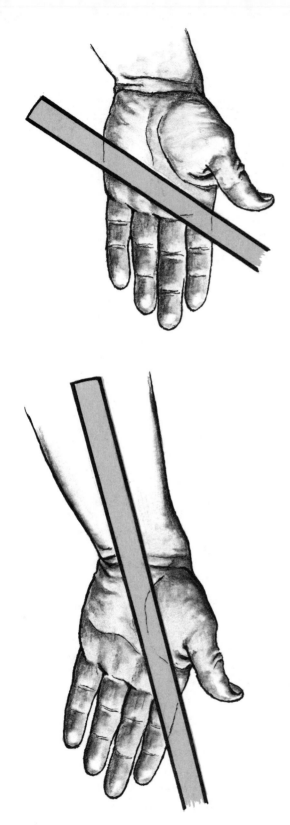

Laying the clubshaft under the heel pad of the left hand (top left illustration) is fine for full swings where the wrists should be allowed to cock and uncock. For wrist-free putting, however, it is better to run the shaft upward between the heel and thumb pads, along the life line on the palm. This positioning not only inhibits wrist action but also allows extending the shaft up against the forearm, as described in the text, to eliminate wrist play.

against the inner portion of your left forearm (see illustration).

Next make a few practice strokes, during which the putter *never* loses contact with your forearm, even during the follow-through.

Finally, position your right hand below the left and actually putt. So long as you retain contact between putter and left forearm, you will make a wrist-free putting stroke. After each putt, check for this contact.

As you putt this way, sense how your arms feel (perhaps like pendulums?). Feel your left arm move away from your side during your follow-through. Then try to duplicate these feelings when your hands are not so far down the shaft, and it is not touching the forearm at address.

Some golfers can adapt to a wrist-free stroke after working with this drill for just a few minutes. Many must pursue it, perhaps on alternate attempts, over a longer period, or before and occasionally during each practice session.

I have found that some pupils putt so well with the shaft against the forearm that they continue to do so indefinitely, even during competition. I do not discourage this practice, but rather encourage it. As they say, it's not *how* that matters; it's *how many*.

Bobby
Locke

Jack
Nicklaus

Billy Casper

Tom Watson

G. Ravielli

15

If you want your putting to be
better than good, you may need
to . . .

Groove your stroke on the inside path

During each of the last several years, I have taught putting to some 300-500 players. It's always risky to stereotype golfers, but I do believe this sampling is sufficient to indicate a particular difference between bad putters, good putters and great putters.

Golfers who vary the path on which they swing the putterhead from putt to putt are usually bad putters. They roll the ball off line in a self-confusing variety of directions. They also have trouble rolling it the right distance.

Those who swing on a *consistent* but *incorrect* path are often surprisingly good putters. At least they have a pattern to their putting. They err the same way most of the time, especially if they practice enough to groove the error(s).

Thus, it is usually better to swing on the same *wrong* path *all the time* than on the *right* path *occasionally.*

But putting on the wrong path all the time is limiting, for at least one simple reason: If your putter is moving in the wrong direction when it meets the ball, the ball will roll in the wrong direction *unless* you face the putter in an offsetting direction.

Consistently swinging to the left of your intended putting line, for instance, requires that you contact the ball with the putter facing to the right of that directional path.

Obviously this creates a glancing blow—putter moving left while facing right.

Moreover, if the path is a consistent *degree* to the left on putt after putt, the club must face a consistent degree to the right. If the difference between path direction and facing is not consistent, the degree that the blow is glancing will vary.

This makes judging distance quite tricky and confusing. If the contact on one putt is extremely glancing, the ball will finish well short of the hole. Naturally the player strikes his next putt more forcefully. If the contact is less glancing this time, the ball rolls too far. Soon the player is in a quandary.

Some golfers do have the talent to swing on more or less the same incorrect path every time while facing the putter to the same offsetting degree. These are often good—not great—putters. They have found a way to make two wrongs—path and blade alignment—produce a fairly useful right.

The great putters are those who swing on a consistent path that is also the correct path. They strike the ball solidly along the line they have chosen. Because the contact is solid and consistent, they have a sound basis on which to build a feel for distance.

These players are usually confident and successful readers of greens, because solid putting makes careful green-reading even more rewarding.

And these players seldom suffer from putting nerves—sound technique creates success, and success creates enough confidence to minimize or disallow nervous tension.

Obviously, swinging the putter consistently on the correct path saves strokes. What is the correct path? I believe it is the path that causes the putter to be:

1. *Moving* down the line you have chosen—"on line," as we say—at the instant it meets the ball.

2. *Facing* down that line—"square" to it—when you swing *naturally*.

We can rule out one path immediately. When the putterhead approaches the ball from outside, or beyond, your chosen line, it cannot possibly move on line at contact. It must move across that line from outside it to inside it, from right to left.

The only two paths that allow us to move the putter on line at contact are (1) straight back and straight forward, with the putterhead never leaving the line, or (2) from inside to along the line.

At first glance it might seem that swinging straight back and forward is the best choice. This might be the best were it not for the fact that we do stand to the side of the ball when putting, just as we do on full shots.

When making a full swing, it would be totally unnatural to move the clubhead on line throughout. It is somewhat unnatural to do so on putts.

Because of our standing to the side, the putter "wants" to move around to the inside on the backswing, though to a far lesser extent than on full swings. On very short putts, it may not want to move off the line at all. But as the need for a longer backswing increases with the distance of the putt, so does the need to let the putterhead depart from the line slightly. On-line swinging starts to become unnatural on putts of more than 6-8 feet, as a general rule, given flat terrain and greens of average speed.

Apart from it being unnatural to force the putter to stay on line on longer putts, doing so also increases the risk of moving it *outside* the line.

It is also unnatural to force the putter to remain

facing in the same direction throughout the putting stroke. Again as in the full swing, the clubhead "wants" to turn clockwise during the backswing and counterclockwise during the forward swing. This natural turning, however, is less likely to happen when the putting stroke is on line throughout.

Now, to summarize:

●Putting on the same path, albeit incorrect, is better than putting on varying paths. But putting on the same correct path is better than putting on the same incorrect path.

●Putting across the line from outside to inside requires a glancing blow of consistent degree and is therefore undesirable. I should add that out-to-in swinging also makes the putter move too steeply downward to the ball, which makes the contact still more glancing.

(Swinging across the line from inside to outside is somewhat less a problem, generally, because the path from the inside is more natural, and the club's angle of approach is not too steeply downward. It does, however, require that the putter be facing to the left of its path at contact. It also enhances the risk of catching grass behind the ball or topping it slightly on the upswing.)

●The straight-back, straight-through path is fine on very short putts where the backswing is just a few inches long. On longer putts, however, it re-

151

quires unnatural manipulation of the club and increases the risk of moving it outside the line.

●The ideal path is straight back and gradually to the inside, then gradually back to and along the line during the forward swing.

Here is a relatively simple way to groove your putting swing on this proper path:

At first, without a ball, practice swinging the putter alongside the baseboard of a wall in your home or a 2x4 board on the putting green.

Start with the toe end of the putter no more than one-half inch from the baseboard or the 2x4. (Using the baseboard can serve an additional purpose; by setting up with the top of your head touching the wall, your eyes will be where they should be—directly over the putting line.)

On each swing try to make the putterhead gradually move a bit farther away from the board during your backswing, and then back to and through its original position.

At first you will probably strike the board with your putter at some point in your swing. Keep swinging until you seldom do.

On your early tries, you will tend to guide the club and flinch for fear of hitting the board. This will make your grip pressure become too tight. Again, continue swinging until you can do so freely without tightening your hands.

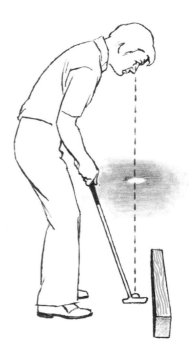

Practicing one's stroke alongside a wall or a board are excellent ways to groove a correct path. Note that the toe of the putter moves slightly away from the wall or board during the backstroke while the facing of the blade remains square to this path throughout.

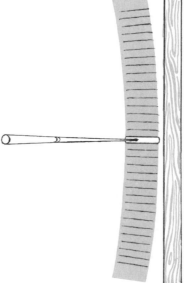

Once you begin to see that the putter is moving on the right path and you are no longer flinching, start trying to sense how your swing feels. The end purpose of this drill is to groove the correct path to the extent that it occurs without your thinking about it, so that you can direct your attention, instead, to the other important matter of making the ball roll the correct distance.

The final step in the drill is to actually putt balls from alongside the board, still starting with the toe end of the putter no more than one-half inch from it.

This particular drill may improve your putting immediately. I must add, however, that finding and *maintaining* the correct putting path requires both immediate and ongoing attention. If you can find at least three or four minutes every day or two to perform this drill, it might well prove to be the single most efficient way of all to improve your golf scores.

Finding wheat amid the chaff

How many different golf professionals have you seen for lessons? How many different books have you read on how to play the game? How many magazine articles? Newspaper tips? How often have you accepted advice from a well-meaning friend?

Golfers, more than any other type of athlete, have been swamped with information, buried under heaps of help.

Then why is it that most of our truly outstanding players have either found a way to play more or less on their own or largely through counsel from a single teacher?

Hagen, Sarazen, Jones, Hogan, Snead, Locke, Palmer, Nicklaus, Trevino, Watson—the list of those

157

who refused to tamper too much with what they had is long indeed.

So too is the list of players with exceptional talents who hopscotched from teacher to teacher, and who never found A WAY that let them win consistently, if at all.

I recall one such player who approached me during a British Open and asked if I would mind watching him take a lesson from "someone else" the next day, "just to make sure what he tells me is right." For his own good, I politely refused, and suggested he settle down with one teacher once and for all.

Anyone who teaches golf, whether he realizes it or not, is governed by certain physical "laws." If the pupil slices his long shots, for instance, one law that applies is that long shots will curve to the right if, during impact, the club is facing to the right of the direction it is moving. To cure that student's slice, the teacher would be forced to obey this law, to prescribe something that would eliminate the open-faced contact.

However, there are many things he might prescribe, depending on his particular preference for that particular pupil. One teacher might prefer altering the player's grip position. Another might stress a lighter grip. Another might start with improving the pupil's aiming of the club. Another might alter ball position, or weight distribution, or prescribe clubs that are more upright. Some might suggest two or three or four of the above, or something altogether different.

This is not to say that one correction might be better than another, that one teacher might be right and all others wrong. (Though students who jump from teacher to teacher often assume this is the case.)

What it does imply is that, as Eddie Merrins says, "there are many different ways to get to Philadelphia."

Eddie is right, of course. Within certain limits there are many variations of grip, address position and swing that will all, if correctly combined, create a contact between club and ball that obeys all the laws. Except for the fact that they both wear spikes and play right-handed, Lee Trevino and Jack Nicklaus are worlds apart in terms of technique, but they are vastly similar in terms of what their clubhead does to the ball.

Where does this wealth of information and wide variety of approaches leave the poor amateur who needs outside help?

My friend Davis Love makes one excellent suggestion: Seek out the teacher in your area who does the most teaching, whose lesson schedule is well-filled in advance, who spends his or her days teaching how to play rather than selling things to wear.

Beyond that, I suggest you ask yourself one question before accepting any piece of advice, oral or written: "Just how will this particular suggestion help ME improve MY club-ball contact?"

Unless the speaker can answer, or the writer has answered, this question to your satisfaction, you'd better disregard the advice and find someone else who can.

I sincerely hope that in each chapter of this book I have given you the information you need to decide if the particular piece of instruction therein does, in fact, apply to your particular needs. If it does apply, and helps, so much the better.

But even then I would caution that very few things in golf seem to work all the time. Rarely has any player, from Vardon to Nicklaus, maintained top form for more than five or six weeks running. As Jack himself has said, "The only consistent thing about this game is its inconsistency."

Moreover, the golf gods tend to react violently when they hear someone say, "I've found the secret."

There are no secrets, no magic moves that will guarantee everlasting success. There are only "keys," as Sam Snead calls them. These are the simple things that help you regain your stride during the dark times.

Hopefully, some of the things I've suggested in this book will become your keys in the years ahead, to help you recapture or strengthen the feeling of what you should be doing in your golf game.